336.2
St2

71677

STATE AND LOCAL TAX PROBLEMS

State and Local Tax Problems

Edited by Harry L. Johnson

KNOXVILLE ⊔ᗠ THE UNIVERSITY OF TENNESSEE PRESS

FOREWORD

IT IS A PLEASURE to introduce this *festschrift* in honor of Dr.
Charles P. White. Although it was not my good fortune to sit
in his classroom, I have known and worked with this distinguished
scholar for more than a quarter of a century at The University of
Tennessee where he has directed the Bureau of Business and
Economic Research with distinction.

Dr. White, a native of Missouri, received his A.B. degree from
Park College in 1920 and the M.A. and Ph.D. degrees from the
University of Pennsylvania where he served as an instructor in
economics from 1921 to 1928. He joined the faculty of The University of Tennessee as associate professor of economics in 1928.

Dr. White has served The University of Tennessee in many and
varied ways, but he is best known for his teaching, research, and
interest in public finance and taxation. In the classroom, Dr.
White has had an obvious and acknowledged impact on the development of ideas and students. Beyond the classroom, his
services to both state and local governments in Tennessee have
been unsurpassed. He has acted as consultant to various Tennessee legislative committees and special commissions investigating
state financial problems. He has been a member of the State
Educational Finance Research Committee, the advisory committee for the Legislative Council Survey of Property Tax Assessment, chairman of the Committee on Public School Finance for
the Survey of Public Education, and financial consultant for the
State Highway Commission. His writings on public finance and
fiscal problems are numerous.

In the early years of the Bureau of Business and Economic Research, it was my privilege to work with Dr. White, adding my
efforts for research in governmental accounting to his outstanding
research abilities in the field of finance. In those days—and nights
—of working together was born a friendship that I have prized
through the years. And in later years as we went our separate ways
in college administration, those early days of exposure to Charlie

White's financial genius served as an inspiration and guide for my own efforts.

Dr. White's long and illustrious career at U.T. has not been confined solely to the fields of research and public service. As a teacher, he was among the best. He became professor of finance in 1935 and served as chairman of the Finance Department until recently when he asked to be released from administrative duties. From the inception of graduate work in the College of Business Administration, he served as director of graduate studies; and the eminence which this program has attained is a credit to his leadership.

It is especially gratifying that the thirty-nine years of service rendered by Dr. White have been recognized by several significant gestures in recent years. Among the highly deserved honors that have been bestowed upon him are election as Phi Kappa Phi Faculty Lecturer at U.T. in 1958 and as Alumni Distinguished Service Professor in 1963. In 1954 his alma mater, Park College, honored him with election as a Distinguished Alumnus. Most recently, Dr. White was honored by this symposium on state and local tax problems, held at the University in May of 1967 and sponsored by the College of Business Administration.

Now that Dr. White is retiring from the active scene, one could grow sentimental and say that the University he has served so long and so well will never be the same again—and let it go at that. To be sure, the University will never be the same again. It will be better in the years ahead—simply because it is building upon the hard work and selfless contributions of men like Charles White.

W. Harold Read
Vice President for Finance, and
Professor of Accounting
The University of Tennessee

PREFACE

THE FINANCING of state and local governments is one of the more timely and important subjects of contemporary America. As the economy has become more affluent, the demands for public services have multiplied at an increasing rate. For example, in the area of public education, government support originally provided at the primary and elementary levels now extends through the high school and the college levels. These and other enlarged quantities and improved qualities of government services require increasing amounts of revenue.

Historically the property tax has provided the main source of state and local revenue. However, during the past several decades sales, income, and privilege taxes and fees have been employed to produce additional revenues. The use of such taxes, although shifting, diffusing, and spreading the burden of state and local finance, has produced a very complex tax structure. As the need for increased state and local expenditure grows, it becomes more and more obvious that finding new sources of revenue and effecting tax revision are mandatory.

The purpose of this volume is twofold. First, the essays are prepared as a special tribute to Professor Charles P. White, a renowned scholar who has devoted his career to the study of state and local tax problems. The authors who have contributed essays are either personal and/or professional friends of Professor White. Each considered this a welcome opportunity to honor one of Tennessee's favorite adopted sons. Second, the book offers several proposals for the solution of contemporary state and local tax problems because the essays are devoted to various aspects of the revenue problem confronted by state and local governments.

A grouping of the essays by subject matter creates four divisions. The lead essay, and the only one in the first division, serves as an introduction in that it establishes a framework for the other essays. Written by Professor James M. Buchanan, it explores the political and fiscal structure of American federalism and suggests that the fiscal and financial problems facing state and local governments are either a direct or an indirect result of the federal progressive income tax system.

The second group of essays concentrates on problems relating to the taxation of property. The introductory essay develops the thesis that the property tax system must undergo revision if it is to continue as a major source of revenue for state and local governments. Modification of the property tax requires administrative as well as base and rate adjustments so that it will more adequately reflect the environmental setting of an urbanized economy. These and other major changes in the property tax are next summarized in Professor Arthur Becker's essay. The major defects pinpointed in this essay relate to assessment, payment and collection, and erosion of the property tax base. Considerable improvement would result from equalization of assessments and the payment of property taxes through monthly installments. Special concessions and lack of administrative rigor have contributed to a deterioration in the property tax base. Exemptions for various institutions, businesses, and classes of individuals have led to a multiplicity of property tax categories and administrative procedures. The shortcomings of the property tax as revealed in Professor Becker's essay are illustrated and documented by Professor C. H. Donovan in his essay on the history of property taxes in Florida. State and local governments in Florida have employed the property tax as a fiscal stimulant as well as a source of revenue.

The third group of essays delineates the economic and political arguments for federal-state-local government tax sharing. Professor Deil Wright establishes the tone of the argument by discussing the need for improvement of the existing federal system of grants to state and local governments. He also provides a description of two major alternatives to the present system—tax credits and tax sharing. Regardless of the system chosen, equalization should be the major objective in revenue sharing. Simplicity, attractiveness, and political sponsorship must characterize the plan chosen to accomplish this aim. The second essay suggests that tax sharing is a must in that the property tax system cannot survive under current and prospective financial conditions of state and local governments. State and local sharing of federal revenues provides the only reasonable solution to these financial problems. The mechanical aspects of the ways in which the federal government may strengthen state and local financing are explored in the essay by Dr. John Shannon, who suggests a system of positive and negative tax credits which will reduce the regressiveness of state and local taxes. This will make sales and property taxes more equitable sources of revenue for state and local governments.

The final essay in this section projects the future fiscal activities of state and local governments. As the level of gross national product continues to expand, the level of state and local expenditures will tend to rise at an increasing rate. The causes of this growth are three: expansion of existing services for a larger population; improvement of the quality of public services; and creation of new and expansion of existing federal-state-local services, *i.e.*, medicare, schools, welfare programs.

Section four contains three essays that explore special financial problems of state and local governments. The first essay considers the question of debt financing. As our population grows, state and local governments will be called upon to provide increasing quantities of services. Some of these should be financed on a "pay-as-you-go" basis. Others, however, will and should be financed through debt. As the volume of state and local debt grows, debt management must be the first order of business. Statutes must be revised and updated so that states may develop a debt policy that promotes economic advance and equity to taxpayers. Necessity should not be the stimulant for debt financing. This essay builds a strong case for the development of financial planning in state and local governments.

Following the discussion of debt and financial planning, Professor James W. Martin explores the problem of assessing the value of public utility property. He argues that the capitalization-of-earnings approach provides the best estimation of public utility property values. Such a method has the attribute of being more accurate than the summation or comparative approach. But although the capitalization approach has proven to be superior, there are two fundamental weaknesses that must be reckoned with: deciding which earnings should be employed and choosing the rate at which earnings should be capitalized.

The concluding essay in this section is devoted to a discussion of financing certain public services by means of service charges. Service charges contribute to efficiency in the use and development of service facilities and shift costs of service directly to users. A major disadvantage of service charges stems from their regressive nature. Although this seems to place service charges at odds with the redistributive objective of taxation, it is suggested that regressivity may be mitigated through an improved application of the service charge principle.

The essays contained in this volume are unique in that they explore a timely and controversial subject—the revenue problems of state and local governments. These governments have experienced increasing difficulties as expenditures have tended to grow faster than revenue. Over a period of time this discrepancy has made it obvious that reform of tax structures and development of new revenue sources are in order. There is agreement that increased revenue is required to finance the expanding programs of state and local governments. Moreover, there is agreement that the federal income tax must provide the major source of increased state and local revenue. Although some sort of revenue sharing system seems to be required, the nature and form that such a system should take remain controversial. The suggestions and descriptions range from a pro rata redistribution of a portion of the revenue collected by the federal government to a closely regulated grant-in-aid program.

Professor James M. Buchanan advocates decreasing the role of the federal government and increasing the role of state-local governments. As social and economic adjustments have enlarged the system of grants-in-aid, the power of the state governments in relation to the federal government has declined. In fact, the future of federalism is threatened. Ideally, this trend could be reversed through a system of programed reductions in federal tax revenue. The programed reductions in federal revenue should be returned to the state-local governments. Such a system would assure state-local governments access to the growth-induced revenues of the progressive income tax. Also, a continuing reduction in federal revenue would promote more responsible fiscal management and limit the federal government's role in the public sector. Such a system would increase the fiscal capacities of state-local units. A net redistribution from the rich to poor states could equalize the fiscal capacities of state-local governments.

The theoretical argument for fiscal equity presented by Professor Buchanan is supported by Professors Wright and Netzer. They, however, tend to support the Heller-Pechman plan, which calls for per capita grants from the federal to state governments. This plan is viewed as having those attributes (simplicity, equalization, flexibility, progressiveness) that are deemed necessary for a federal-state-local government revenue sharing program. Professor Wright, a political scientist, tends to view the problem as having indisputable economic justifications but only limited appeal to politicians. He feels that some form of a federal-state-local government revenue sharing system will be established. Such a system must, however, be simple, be attractive to state and local political leaders, and have national political party support.

Professor Netzer, on the other hand, suggests that the inherent weaknesses of the property tax system will force the creation of a federal-state-local revenue sharing system. Administrative problems, social and economic objectives, location of economic activity, growth of public service are forces which require a simple and flexible source of revenue. A federal tax sharing program is a necessary innovation to preserve American federalism.

Reform of the property tax system cannot solve the revenue

needs of state-local governments. It can, however, contribute to enlarged sources of revenue for local governments. The greatest advantages to be derived from property tax reform are equity and administrative efficiency. History illustrates that it cannot serve as a source of increased revenue to finance enlarged state-local expenditures. Alterations in assessment, applicability, and method of collecting property taxes could, however, increase the amount of revenue derived from the property tax. The essays of this volume advocate equalization of assessment, the elimination of special categories of property, and the reduction, if not the elimination, of special exemptions. Professor Becker is bold enough to propose a revolutionary innovation in the collection of the property tax. A monthly installment system administered by the federal government could enhance and greatly improve the receipt of tax revenues by state-local governments. He argues that property owners would find this a more convenient and less painful method of paying property taxes.

To a significant extent these objectives are already being achieved by means of the existing escrow system which applies to the bulk of mortgaged property. There would appear to be little need to substitute federal machinery for an already existing system that seems efficient. It would be a simple matter to implement legislation requiring the transfer of monthly payments from tax escrow accounts to the local taxing authority. Where the escrow system does not apply, the monthly payment could be included as a component of the bill which the taxpayer receives for utility or other sources sold on a monthly basis.

In this connection it is interesting to note Professor Kafoglis' suggestion that an expanded system of service charges could be developed as a partial substitute for general property taxes. Such a system would serve to achieve Professor Becker's objective of monthly revenue receipts, would encourage efficiency in the development and use of local services, and might lead to a reduction of the pressure on the general property tax system. These ideas for radical changes highlight the rigidity and lack of imagination that have historically characterized the administration of local tax systems.

A thoughtful consideration of these essays will reveal that the discovery of adequate revenue sources is not in itself a sufficient solution to the present problem. The development of fiscal institutions consistent with the maintenance of a viable federalism seems essential and, in the long run, may prove to be the most difficult part of the task.

H.L.J.

CONTENTS

LIST OF TABLES

PART ONE

Introduction

FINANCING A VIABLE FEDERALISM

James M. Buchanan

Most americans are pragmatists. Their civilization reflects this virtue; it also exhibits this vice. They are masters of "muddling through," of "fixing things up" (baling wire should be the American symbol). Most Americans do not now think, nor have they thought for a century, in terms of "structures," of "systems," of "societies." Despite the slogans, the New Deal, the New Frontier, the Great Society were, and are, mere patchworks of politically oriented responses to emergent needs, real or manufactured.

To this dominant American mentality, "the constitution" is an alien concept. The idea that there should exist rules and institutions explicitly chosen for the purpose of guaranteeing orderly processes of change in unknown directions runs counter to pragmatist persuasion. The latter concentrates on the particular problem in the here and now. The constitutional emphasis on the institutions under which problems may be met—any problems that arise—now and in the long term seems an aberration.

Nowhere is this pragmatic approach more sharply evidenced than in discussions of the federal political structure. Political pragmatists are rarely interested in principles of political order; they seek only to meet each problem as it arises and to twist existing institutions as they must to get results. They cannot understand the occasional constitutionalist, who does espouse a basic principle. When the latter raises a warning cry, if ever so feebly, about the dangers of an ever increasing centralization of political power, the pragmatist sees, not a reasoned defense of principle but instead, reaction against progress itself.

It is fitting that my contribution to this volume be devoted to aspects of intergovernmental fiscal relations. My own career as an economist effectively commenced with my apprenticeship under Dr. Charles P. White in 1940–41 when I worked explicitly on state-local revenue sharing.

Today, the pragmatists are more numerous than ever before. The episodic 1964 attempt of Senator Goldwater to force a national discussion on principles was swamped in irrelevancy, almost before it started. The few faint signs of an awakened public awareness of the federal principle that the radically irresponsible reapportionment decisions aroused have long since faded into nothingness. The majority of the Warren court is pragmatism writ supreme, determined to move America forward decision by decision to "better" things, as chosen by its own moral (or glandular) responses, and blissfully ignorant of the essential and elemental meaning of either federalism or of constitutionalism.

Sober prediction must indeed be somber. Few can view with unconcern the increasing centralization of political power that we witness. But lacking a base in principle, the pragmatist acquiesces and hopes that excesses will be few. He sees no satisfactory alternative to the developing unitary state, and he has not been impressed by modern-day Calhouns. He knows, intuitively, that the federal bureaucracy must grow ever larger, relatively and absolutely, and that more and more federal action will impinge both on traditional state-local and on individual responsibility.

Effective leadership is desperately required; yet by its very nature pragmatism produces none. Leadership requires vision, a look beyond the here and now, a look at the structure of society itself, an argument from first principle. Failing such leadership, Americans wallow in their prosperous discontent, afraid to support positive action because they do not understand the logic of political organization itself.

Nothing is more urgent than a forced opening up of perspective. Must Americans acquiesce silently in the emergence of the unitized society, dominated from Washington by the inherent mediocrities of massive bureaucracy? Or is it yet possible to resort to traditional American skills in patching things up so that demands for new public programs can be met as these materialize while at the same time preserving the essential values of decentralized political and economic power?

4

Toward Institutional Understanding

Why did we witness, especially during the 1950's when a conservative administration held executive power, a continued and even accelerated proliferation of federal nondefense spending programs, many of which took the form of conditional matching grants-in-aid to states and localities? Why must we, as detached observers, predict similar expansion during the last half of the 1960's and beyond?

The relative growth in federal nondefense outlay is due to one basic cause: the federal income tax. The year 1913 is one of the most significant in the history of the American federal structure. With the adoption of the Sixteenth Amendment to the Constitution, the central government was granted access to the single fiscal weapon that was to remake the whole national fiscal pattern. This was not recognized at the time, and such consequences were not even remotely in the minds of those who supported the amendment. Omniscient indeed would have been the man who, in 1913, could have predicted the future growth in either national income or the relative importance of the public sector. And, lacking such omniscience, who could have foreseen the transformation of the income tax into one of the most productive revenue yielders in all history?

Only within recent years, and notably since 1960, have economists come to realize fully the effects of continuous growth in national income and product on the relative productivities of the traditional fiscal instruments. The highly progressive rate structure of the income tax guarantees that national income growth will produce more than proportionate increases in revenue yield. This remains true whether the growth be illusory because of inflation or real because of a growth in the output of goods and services. As the national economy grows, the revenues flowing into the federal treasury must grow more than proportionately, given the existing institutional structure. It is estimated that, without further changes in federal tax rates, an additional $10 to $15 bil-

5

lion will be produced each year over the next half-decade, provided only that growth persists in the national economy.

In contrast to this built-in producer of additional revenue which the central government possesses, the states and local units are poor indeed. They can, and many do, levy taxes on income. But these taxes cannot be highly progressive because of the free flow of men and materials over the whole economy. At best, a limited amount of net redistribution can be implemented at state-local levels. Income tax rates must be low and not highly progressive. Major reliance must be placed on sales taxation at the state level, and on property taxation at the local level. These sources of revenue have proved to be much more expansive during the postwar period than many scholars had earlier predicted. But they remain second-rate when stacked up against the federal income tax, personal and corporate.

Once these few fiscal facts are recognized, an understanding of what we have witnessed is achieved. Elected politicians, both legislative and executive, know intuitively that votes, and re-elections, are gained by reducing taxes on the one hand and by expanding spending on the other. Votes are lost by increasing tax rates and by cutting down spending programs. This basic fiscal asymmetry is acknowledged by even the most abstract idealist who looks at political process in a democracy. This asymmetry alone will not, however, explain the apparent proclivity of federal politicians to approve a lengthening list of new spending programs. One additional step is required, and this is provided by the recognition that more votes may be gained by expanding spending than by cutting taxes, provided matching provisions can be required that call forth more than dollar-for-dollar spending on the part of states and localities.

Look briefly at the position of the individual legislator who is asked to give his support to a new program for a matching grant-in-aid. The approval of the program will not require increased federal tax rates, due to the built-in increase in yield. No votes need be lost here. The alternatives to the grant-in-aid may be a reduction in federal taxes (the one chosen in 1964) or an increase in direct federal spending. The legislator will be strongly tempted to choose the grant-in-aid since, by so doing, he may claim credit for the full effects of a spending program that is only partially financed out of federal revenues.

This institutional explanation of what we observe is not, of course, the familiar one. Instead, we find explanations familiarly running in terms of the emerging and accelerating "needs" of the states and localities for new programs of spending, along with the inability of these units to raise sufficient revenues independently. These explanations seem superficially plausible, until it is recognized that they do not "explain" anything at all. What does "inability to finance needed services" mean? Literally, it suggests only that state-local politicians are unwilling to raise additional tax revenues to support additional spending programs. The so-called greater ability of the central government stems almost exclusively from the built-in revenue increments under the income tax, which, translated into decision terms, means that new programs may be financed without the necessity of levying new taxes.

Given the institutions as they exist, and given the proclivities of politicians to act like the ordinary men they are, what is wrong with merely leaving things alone? What is wrong with a policy of laissez-faire? If it is easier to meet the demands of citizens for spending programs by allowing new federal grants-in-aid to be the implementing devices, why should we worry? Is not the immediate task that of getting the job done? There may, of course, be some gnawing concern that the citizen of Baltimore really is not interested in urban renewal in Tacoma, but, after all, why should he worry so long as Baltimore also qualifies for the same largesse.

This is precisely the pragmatic state of mind; and it is this refusal to take the larger perspective that forestalls support, or even discussion, of positive institutional reforms. The laissez-faire outcome is unacceptable because it allows the fiscal structure to

7

distort the constitutional division of powers between the central government and the states. The problem is one of principle, and principle must be adduced for rational discussion.

The Federal Principle

Philosophers long dead have possessed both the wisdom and the courage to examine issues that modern man ignores at his folly. At base, the central issue concerns man's power over man. This issue, as complex in solution as it is simple in statement, is worthy of man's most profound reflection, be it now or in the eighteenth century. How shall man so organize his political and economic institutions as to limit the power of one individual over another? This is the specific question that we shun, and that the Founding Fathers faced explicitly.

The United States, as we know its history, is *their construction*. The foundations have proved sturdy ones, capable of supporting much of which these practical philosophers never dreamed. The principle upon which all else rests is that of *limiting power concentration through decentralization*, through fragmentation, through divisibility. The nation's political order was designed in a *federal* pattern, with political sovereignty divided between the central government and the separate states. The constitutional division, with powers explicitly delegated to the central government and residual powers given to the states, was not designed with efficiency in mind, for efficiency always raises criteria questions. The constitutional division of powers was aimed at limiting the central government, the only arm of government that has no competitors, the only unit from which migration is not readily available.

The economic order was conceived in the same way, and the close similarity between the federal political structure and a competitive or free enterprise economy seems rarely to have been understood. The market economy is a means of decentralizing political power, since in so far as this economy organizes resources with tolerable efficiency, decisions need not be made politically. As the Soviets are belatedly discovering, decentralization also

8

makes for economic efficiency, but to base the central argument for a market economy on simple efficiency grounds is a gross distortion of the lesson that Adam Smith tried to teach us all.

But the pragmatist is impatient with principle. He rarely resorts to counterprinciple. Few are those who forthrightly argue for deliberate expansion of central government power, or, more broadly, for concentration of political-economic power, *per se*. The pragmatist, instead, argues in ignorance of principle, either genuine or feigned. He decries resort to what he calls "nineteenth-century argument" against "good" projects and programs "now." He, and those who support him, fail to see, again either innocently or deliberately, that the viability of the whole political-economic order depends critically on some final limits being placed on continued jerry-building. Honest men must at the least be willing to look beyond the single program proposals and to see what sort of social structure they are building. These men may, of course, disagree as to the limits to be drawn, as to the current dangers of centralized power, as to the costs and the benefits of particular programs. But the debate deserves better than modern Americans have given it. The federal principle does not deserve burial by default; it warrants the elemental decency of formal funeral.

A few nonpragmatist scholars will argue persuasively that the principle of limiting political power is not applicable today, that both federalism and the market economy are anachronistic carryovers from our inherited past. These scholars should be heard with respect and detachment, and their vision of American society matched against that of those who espouse the federal principle. Having heard both sides, honest men must then adopt their own guidelines. They need not, of course, be extremist in either light. But they must become nonpragmatist to the extent that they understand the relationships between jerry-building and the foundations of social order.

The Effective Alternatives

If the federal principle is accepted, some positive value must be placed on slowing down, if not reversing, the continued erosion of private and state-local government responsibility accompanied by the steady accumulation of central government direction. Given the institutional setting as it exists, this desirable objective cannot be accomplished through a simple act of national will. Fundamental institutional reform will be necessary, reform that is designed to remove from central government politicians, in both the executive and the legislative branches, the opportunity they now possess to inaugurate new spending programs without the offsetting responsibility of levying new taxes. In addition, this reform must, in some fashion, guarantee that access to the progressive income tax, to its growth-induced revenue yield, be made available to state-local units. There are several alternative reforms which will accomplish this purpose in different ways.

Programed Federal Tax Reduction. If a long-range and planned program for continuing reduction in the level of federal tax rates should be put into effect, the invitation to irresponsibility placed before federal politicians would be removed to an extent. If, in advance, expectations came to be based on the knowledge that federal tax rates would be reduced each year roughly commensurate with the built-in increase in revenues, the ease with which new programs for spending might be inaugurated would be partially eliminated. The President and the Congress would then find it necessary to increase the deficit, to raise other taxes, or to forego the anticipated rate reduction, if new spending plans are enacted.

This reform has much to recommend it. Few serious objections were raised to the similar proposal made by Senator Goldwater during the 1964 campaign. The main objection that was voiced, and mostly by journalists and not economists, centered on the plan's restrictions on the flexibility of adjustments in the federal budget. But, of course, the removal of such flexibility, and its replacement by a predictable institutional rule upon which firm expectations could be based, is precisely the plan's virtue to one who accepts the federal principle.

A more serious objection that may be made to this reform concerns its onesidedness. It aims primarily at restricting the built-in bias toward overspending by the central government, but it does little to expand the fiscal base for states and localities. Indirectly, of course, these units would be strengthened. They would surely find it increasingly less difficult to raise tax rates. Practically, however, this would remain a formidable task, and few would predict that state-local revenues would be increased sufficiently to offset fully the gradual reduction in federal collections.

This reform appeals to those whose value judgments support, generally, a reduction in the share of national resources organized through the public sector, at all levels. Its shortcomings are noted by those whose concern lies primarily, not with the overall public sector–private sector mix, but with the disproportionate central government share in the public sphere. To this second group of supporters of the federal principle, programed federal tax reduction is at best a half-way measure. This reform will not, of course, prove at all acceptable to those who support neither a reduction in the proportionate share of resources organized publicly, nor an increase in spending by states and localities relative to the central government.

Aside from its failure to strengthen explicitly the revenue base of states and localities, programed reduction in federal tax rates raises a second serious objection, but one that is perhaps less widely shared than the first. The federal income tax is the major revenue producer in the American fiscal structure, and this tax contains within it great potential for disproportionate revenue increases as the national economy grows. In part for the same reason, this tax is also the primary means through which net income redistribution is accomplished via the fiscal mechanism. Through its financing a major share of programs that provide either general benefits to the population or benefits that are unrelated to taxes paid, this tax generates a post-tax, post-benefit real income distribution that is significantly more equal than the pre-tax, pre-benefit one. Any net reduction in collections from the federal income tax, even if the same rate of progressivity is maintained, and even if

11

revenue losses are fully offset by increased state-local collections, will serve to reduce the redistributive potential of the whole system. This result arises from the limitation that the openness of the national economy places on net redistribution at the state-local levels. Any such unit that exceeds rather narrow limits in transferring funds from its rich to its poor must face an out-migration of its wealthy and an in-migration of indigents.

This redistributive objection to programed reduction in federal tax rates is a valid one, but it has less weight than casual consideration suggests. Such a reform would, at best, be aimed at holding federal collections roughly at current levels; more realistically, all that would be accomplished would be some reduction in the rate of increase in federal revenues. At most, therefore, the reform would inhibit further shifts toward additional redistribution in the federal fiscal structure. It would pose no threat to continuing current patterns of redistribution. When this point is accepted, along with the declining need for redistributive measures in an economy where all income rises over a period of time, the objection seems to be of limited significance.

Once defense-spending levels are stabilized, programed reduction in federal tax rates would be politically and administratively feasible. Few practical difficulties should arise in a plan which would call for, say, a reduction in federal income tax rates by 4 or 5 per cent annually over a period of four, five, or ten years. Disagreement might, of course, arise as to the precise manner of the reduction and as to the specific percentage amounts. At the one extreme, an attempt could be made to reduce federal collections roughly commensurate with revenue growth, thus making gross federal collections stable as time passes. More realistically, an attempt could be made to build into the structure a device that would force the central government to relinquish, on a predictable basis, only a specified share of the increase in revenue yield. For fiscal 1965, the federal income tax, personal and corporate, yielded roughly $75 billion. A programed reduction of 5 per cent annually in collections from this tax would still allow federal budgetary revenues to grow more than $2 billion annually, provided that the economy grows. A 4 per cent annual reduction would allow for a $3 billion annual growth in federal budgetary revenues, roughly splitting the increment between budgetary increases and reduced collections.

The difficulties of this reform are those of maintaining fiscal discipline over any period of programed reduction. As the history of the so-called "temporary" taxes has demonstrated, temptations would mount to depart from announced reduction plans, provided that newly popular spending proposals emerge which demand new financing. To be effective, any long-range tax reduction program should be institutionalized to the maximum extent possible.

Tax Sharing. A second reform that would effectively meet the same objections is one that calls for some sharing of federal income tax collections with the states. In this scheme, there would be no planned reduction in federal tax rates over any period of time. Instead, a specified, and presumably increasing, share of federal revenue collections would be returned directly to the states where such revenues are originally collected. The states would be allowed to share in the tax, as levied and collected by the central government.

This alternative has a major advantage over the first one examined in that the reduction in federal revenue expansion is simultaneously accompanied by a strengthening of the state revenue base. States and localities may, of course, choose to cut their own taxes rather than to expand expenditures by the full amount of the federally returned shares. It seems clear, however, that major increases in state-local spending on almost all public services performed at these levels would occur. This alternative appeals directly to those whose primary concern is with the imbalance in the public sector itself, between the fiscal capacity of the central and of the state-local governments.

The second of the basic objections made to programed federal tax reduction continues to be valid in opposition to this scheme, although to a lesser extent. The degree of net redistribution that

13

might be achieved through the fiscal structure is limited, despite the fact that this tax sharing plan will allow for a much greater overall dependence on the progressive income tax than the first plan. However, the redistributive potential on the spending side of the budget will be reduced somewhat below that which would be possible under a simple expansion in central government spending. This is because the return of revenues to state-of-origin would allow for no net redistribution over the geographical areas of the nation. The relatively poor states would receive relatively small shares in returned revenues. Hence, individual citizens of such states would be under heavier fiscal pressures than their equals in the rich states. Administratively, this may be corrected through the establishment of arbitrary rules which would serve to determine the appropriate shares by state-of-origin.

Equalizing Bloc Grants. There remains a third basic reform which could accomplish the objective of countering the built-in bias toward central government fiscal growth yet strengthen the fiscal bases of state-local units and allow for any desired degree of net income-wealth redistribution through the whole structure. This is the reform that has been discussed under the name of the "Heller plan," and, apparently, was central in the proposals of the 1964 Pechman Task Force Report. This reform involves the return to the states of a share of federal revenues, allocated in accordance with some simple, readily understandable sharing formula.

This alternative would accomplish three things. First, the central government would be limited in its access to the increasing federal revenue kitty. Second, the fiscal capacities of the state-local units would be increased in direct relationship to decreases in federal potential. Third, through some sharing scheme, such as equal-per-person totals, a net redistribution from the rich states to the poor states could be implemented. By contrast with this third reform, the programed tax reduction scheme discussed above accomplishes only the first of these. Tax sharing, as outlined, also accomplishes the second. But only some scheme for equalizing bloc grants accomplishes the third objective.

This fundamental reform in the fiscal structure deserves general support by those who accept the relevance of the federal principle, who are concerned with an overexpansion in spending at the federal level, who desire additional outlays on public services at state-local levels, and who support, generally, some plan for equalizing the fiscal capacities among the several states. This reform will be opposed by two groups: first, by those who want to restrict public spending at all levels, and who want to limit severely the redistributive potential of the whole fiscal structure; second, by those who want to expand public spending, especially at the central government level, and who consider states and localities incapable of making "good" decisions on their own. Since these two groups can, in a rough sense, be classified as falling respectively on the "right" and the "left" along the political-ideological spectrum, support for the third reform should come basically from the broad center of American opinion.

The effectiveness of any system of equalizing bloc grants would be severely weakened by the insertion of restrictions or conditions designed to inhibit state decisions concerning the use of funds. If press reports are accurate, the Pechman Task Force weaseled on its recommendations in this respect. While its argument seems to have been based on an acceptance of the federal principle, it refused to follow its own logic and reportedly recommended certain conditions on the freedom of recipients to spend grants.

A program of equalizing bloc grants, returned directly to the states on some simple sharing formula, seems politically and administratively feasible. Certain press comment subsequent to President Johnson's endorsement of this reform suggested that issues of constitutionality might arise in the making of such grants. This comment was almost surely a smokescreen thrown up by the plan's opponents. Questions of constitutionality are hardly worth discussing at any rate, since the current Supreme Court makes few gestures to constitutional legitimacy. Whether or not this plan, or any other, is "constitutional" depends strictly on whether or not the Court thinks it is "good"—nothing more—and discussions at any other level are wasted words.

As with the other effective alternatives discussed here, disagreement might arise as to the precise totals to be returned under any bloc grant scheme. Press reports suggested that the Pechman Task Force proposed a $2 to $3 billion annual total. Subsequent proposals have varied from $1 billion to some $10 billion in annual totals.

It should be noted that Canada currently combines a system of equalizing bloc grants with a return of income tax shares to provinces of origin, save in exceptional cases for provinces that are not "members" of this scheme. There is, of course, no reason why some combination of all three of the alternatives here discussed could not be implemented.

Second-Best Alternatives

Nonprogramed Reductions in Federal Tax Rates. Although arguments in its support were based on different grounds, the 1964 revenue legislation did represent a single step toward limiting growth in central government spending. If, as tax revenues grow over time, decisions are made to reduce rates, the goals of those who broadly accept the federal principle might be partially achieved. Reliance should not, however, be placed in this type of fiscal action as the 1966–67 experience now demonstrates. The tax reduction of 1964 seems more likely to have been an accident in fiscal history. The disciplined control exhibited in 1963 and 1964 has almost totally disappeared, and spending pressures, defense and otherwise, now swamp other considerations. At best, spasmodic reductions in tax rates must be considered as an indirect and second-best means of maintaining a viable federal polity.

Tax Credits. Various proposals have been made for the introduction of credits against federal income tax payments for payments made by individuals and firms under state-local taxes of specific kinds. These schemes amount to net reductions in federal revenue collections, without a reduction in rate levels, and they would provide strong incentives for state-local units to enact tax legislation aimed at exploiting the credits. Precisely because of this feature, however, tax credits involve federal control of state-local tax decisions, which specifically violates the federal principle. In the final analysis, tax credit schemes seem to be subject to the same objections as federal tax sharing, while generating additional objections of their own. Nevertheless, tax credits should be considered as one part of a broader program aimed at strengthening a federal fiscal structure.

False Alternative: Conditional Grants-in-Aid

The alternative most likely to be chosen, especially upon cessation of hostilities in Viet Nam, and given the pragmatic state of American opinion, is a proliferation of federal grant-in-aid programs, through which the swelling federal revenue stream is channeled into areas of public spending heretofore reserved exclusively for state-local financing and control. As suggested above, the natural proclivity of federal politicians and bureaucrats will be to support this utilization of incremental revenues over all its alternatives. Through this device, they can generate, via matching provisions, a greater than one-for-one expansion in spending on programs which they select and which they can effectively control. In addition, they can pay lip service to the respect for federal principles by explicitly disavowing attempts at control. The conditions to be laid down, they will argue, are very general ones, and genuine decentralization can be preserved in the actual administration of the separate programs.

These arguments must be recognized for what they are. In 1968 it requires no great wisdom or insight to perceive that federal funds transferred to state-local units under grant-in-aid programs must involve control by the federal government. The naive view that such control need not become excessive or dangerous might have been respectably held in 1960, or even in 1962. But the dramatic shift in American attitudes in the years since President Kennedy stated that he did not think the federal executive could or *should* withhold funds from states under duly enacted programs is clear to all. Only the genuine fool can argue that the extension of federal grants-in-aid can proceed without sapping the basic strength of the American federal structure.

But the attractions of this false alternative are many. The state-local politician, like his federal counterpart, sees the opportunity of shifting fiscal responsibility. He willingly trades off his budgetary freedom for the mess of federal pottage. He fails to recognize that any of the effective alternatives would be vastly superior from his own point of view. Perhaps the most important attraction of this false alternative lies in its ability to meet problems in a piecemeal, one-at-a-time fashion. The politicians can respond to the needs of the separate pressure groups by setting up new programs without raising, or even discussing, questions of constitutional principle. State-local functions are not assumed or taken away by the central government, since the latter only provides "grants-in-aid," with a few conditions. The accretion of federal power moves step by step, and state-level units find themselves more and more dependent on federal programs. Even for those who comprehend the larger picture, the merits of particular programs tend to be overwhelming. The "need" for additional spending at state-local levels remains ever large, and largely unmet. All citizens want "better schools, fewer slums, better urban transit, clean water, clean air," provided, of course, they can get all these at a bargain, which federal grant-in-aid programs seem to offer. These "good things" are concrete, tangible, and they can be directly measured in a citizen's psychology of behavior. By contrast, few citizens want "decentralization of power," "state-local control," "limitation of federal control." These are abstractions; these are only remote "good things," and tangible measurement becomes almost impossible to the ordinary man who thinks not on principle at all. Given this prevailing attitude, the self-interested bureaucracy can, of course, generate wide support for particular programs of federal intervention. And it can succeed in bottling up any serious discussion of the alternatives which could, indirectly, secure these same concrete and tangible "goods" without the accompanying intangible "bads."

The bureaucracy will prevail. New and varied programs of grants-in-aid will emerge, all designed to promote "good things," as chosen by the federal establishment, and all to be administered by state-local units under conditions as laid down from on high. The growing federal revenue stream will be tapped, used, and exhausted; and the American federal dream will be pronounced dead by default.

All this is not, of course, foreshadowed in our stars. Effective leadership can promote, even now, a serious discussion of the relevant alternatives. A viable system of decentralized political and economic power can be secured, and strengthened, as a result. The United States can continue to be the United States.

PART TWO

Property Taxes

REFORM OF PROPERTY TAX SYSTEMS:
Substance or Semantics

Arthur D. Lynn, Jr.

IT IS COMMONPLACE, but nonetheless worthwhile, to recall that the property tax is in fact a series of American adaptations of a medieval fiscal arrangement which apparently has been going through a tax-base expansion and contraction cycle, which for convenience I label the Seligman cycle, since time immemorial.[1] While I am by no means a fiscal determinist, this phenomenon reminds one of the long slow cyclical roll of history within which our often myopic short-term evaluations are made.

Bearing in mind the long waves of development, it is also noteworthy that we are now in a period of rapid change in our socioeconomic environment. For the moment it is enough to observe that this shifting environmental context radically affects the technical possibilities for and the political probabilities of tax revision, including property tax policy decisions.

Accordingly, we can ignore neither the importance of rediscovering the already known nor the necessity of recognizing new constraints and expanded opportunities arising from environmental change. This sounds fulsome indeed; for the moment, let me refer to the opinion of that noted tax expert Robert Frost on the nature of desirable change.[2]

> I advocate a semi-revolution.
> The trouble with a total revolution
> (ask any reputable Rosicrucian)
> Is that it brings the same class up on top.
> Executives of skillful execution

---

[1] See my "Property-Tax Development: Selected Historical Perspectives," in Richard W. Lindholm (ed.), *Property Taxation—USA* (Madison: University of Wisconsin Press, 1967).

[2] *Complete Poems of Robert Frost* (New York: Holt, Rinehart & Winston, 1949), 497.

Will therefore plan to go halfway and stop.
Yes, revolutions are the only salves,
But they're one thing that should be done by halves.

This prescription, I submit, has distinct merit for tax policy including property tax policy.

Environmental Conditions

Aside from revolutions not by halves, fiscal institutions are prone to rather slow change; even a major development like modern national fiscal policy required a protracted period for assimilation. The property tax likewise has changed but, as we all know, at a very slow, arthritic, glacial pace. Yet one may still wonder how contemporary change affects the chances of property tax adjustment. To that end, a consideration of some environmental conditions may prove useful.

The property tax developed in a period of both private and public scarcity when agriculture was predominant, transportation and communication were primitive, government was decentralized, international commitments were minimal, and the public sector of the economy was relatively small. Currently, these conditions are all dramatically different—different in ways which place new strains upon the operations of American federalism and modify the context within which tax policy decisions are made and executed. Though selection of the relevant is difficult, the following factors seem significant in relation to property tax reform, from an environmental point of view:

(1) Development of a productive capacity and an uneven affluence which raise simultaneously the hope of banishing scarcity and the specter of a new congeries of social problems.

(2) Variable international commitments—military, political, and economic—which limit to some degree the distributive reality and the effective economic minima of the affluent society.

(3) The rapid urbanization of a science and technologically

dominated society accompanied by shifts in the locus of political power.

(4) Population expansion producing a crowded society and simultaneously the computerization of information handling and the progressive automation of production processes in that society.

(5) The expansion of public sector demand for new and enlarged programs designed to cope with or alleviate contemporary socio-economic problems.

(6) The separation of public sector program expansion requirements—often most acute at the state and local level—and tax levying capacity which is obviously, in a national economy, most effective at the national level.

These significant, but by no means all inclusive, factors materially affect prospects for property tax change and provide the relevant backdrop for considering property tax reform. In no small measure, these interacting factors and others like them should determine the future of that ancient fiscal institution.

Types of Potential Property Tax Modification

As Jensen has said, "If any tax could have been eliminated by adverse criticism, the property tax should have been eliminated long ago." [3] Despite a lengthy series of waves of adverse comment, the diverse set of taxes generally labeled "the property tax" has been singularly resistant to change, which has come at only a glacial rate. Necessity explains the retention of the status quo; but a not unduly Byzantine suspicion arises—could the scholarly consensus be a sterile result of logic uncontaminated by contact with reality? In any event, numerous reforms have been suggested. These appear to fall into five categories, (1) administrative adjustments, (2) shifts in the locus of administrative responsibility,

[3] Jens P. Jensen, *Property Taxation in the United States* (Chicago: University of Chicago Press, 1931), 478.

(3) base and rate adjustments, (4) alternative ways of taxing property, and (5) proposed tax substitutes.

Administrative Adjustments. The most frequently noted administrative deficiency in the property tax is poor organization for an effective performance of the assessment function. Underassessment and non-uniform assessment are and long have been commonplace but nonetheless very significant faults of American property taxation. Logical remedies exist; they have been of record for a long time. In fact, few altogether new ideas about the processes of assessment, review, and equalization are now apparent. It would, perhaps, be quite enough to apply the already known, especially now that their potential is greatly enhanced by modern computer data processing and analytical capabilities.

The conventional wisdom of property tax reform says that assessment administration should be professionalized. Why has this seemingly obvious truth been less than completely applied in practice? Over and over again what has come to be a complex tax in a complex society is given an administrative budget, inadequate by nineteenth-century standards and pathetically ludicrous by those of today. Even if, as is commonly alleged by conventional wags, taxpayers are already receiving more property tax administration than they are paying for (which is often quite true), cost requirements for professionalization and its derivative, effective administration, are not being met, at least not everywhere.

Habit, inertia, hypocrisy, and effective tax reduction and/or low tax maintenance aspirations may explain existing deficiencies. In a larger sense, this sly strategy of tax minimization is self-defeating since it emasculates local government, passes program definition, control, and financing upstairs to state and national governments, complicates federalism, and fails to delineate the scope of the public sector in relation to the objectives of at least some of its proponents. In fact, it has only braked rather than effectively limited property tax liabilities and this at the cost of what may be termed either inequity or, more charitably, extralegal differential classification of property categories and taxpayers.

It is time to decide that effective, honest, even-handed property tax administration is worth its cost, and to pay the bill. Indirect tax limitation resulting from deficient administration is a poor strategy which has high indirect costs and often fails to accomplish its own objectives. As one reporting National Tax Association committee observed, "Our failures are practical failures, failures defined for the most part, by an apparent unwillingness to design the machinery and pay the expenses for the operation of a tax which is, by nature, an extremely difficult one to administer." [4]

Shifts in the Locus of Tax Administrative Responsibility. Historical generalizations about *ad valorem* taxation require cautious expression if minimal accuracy is to be attained. Without undue qualification, however, the property tax can be described as having passed through two more or less concurrent developmental patterns. As far as revenue disposition is concerned, it has become an essentially local tax. At the same time, as property has become more complex and local governmental units less congruent with the present area of effective economic relationships, some administrative responsibilities have been transferred from local to state government agencies. The assessment of public utility property provides a convenient and conventional example of this process.

Since state governments are responsible for the legal framework of their constituent local governments and of their state and local systems of taxation, the states are by definition responsible for their *ad valorem* tax systems. This responsibility has often not been effectively met. Clearly if minimal standards of administration are to be achieved, the states must provide them, either directly or indirectly.

Several years ago the Report on Property Tax Policy by a National Tax Association committee, in commenting upon the Bird Report, which was entitled *The Role of the States in Strengthening the Property Tax*, offered the following summary:

---

[4] Report of the Committee on State Equalization of Local Tax Assessments, *Proceedings of the National Tax Association*, 1958, p. 316.

The Report of the Advisory Commission on Inter-governmental Relations has noted three alternative administrative arrangements for property tax assessment: (1) complete centralization of property tax administration; (2) complete centralization of property tax assessment with tax collection and enforcement handled locally; and (3) well coordinated state-local administration. While this Committee makes no election between these alternatives, it does commend them to policymakers for consideration and suggests that when one approach is selected it should be implemented in a vigorous and effective fashion. At the very least, assessment districts should be combined into large enough units to permit adequate compensation and well trained professional assessment personnel. In addition, state authorities should be enabled to provide local assessors with effective technical and legal assistance and should be given authority to issue appropriate directives having the force of law.[5]

The Bird Report which the National Tax Association Committee was commenting upon recommended:

Centralized assessment administration, with more inclusive centralization when dictated by efficiency, should be considered for immediate adoption by some states and for ultimate adoption by most States. It offers an uncomplicated and effective means of obtaining uniformly high-standard assessing throughout a State by the use of an integrated professional staff following standard methods and procedures under central direction.[6]

These prescriptions seem sound, especially when related to the potentials of modern data processing. The National Tax Association Committee noted in this connection:

Prompt and creative application of modern data processing capabilities to property tax administration offers a substantial opportunity for improving this ancient tax. Enlarged assessment units will assist in making this opportunity functionally available.

[5] Report of the Committee on Model Property Tax Assessment and Equalization Methods on Property Tax Policy, *Proceedings of the National Tax Association*, 1964, p. 157 at 193–4.

[6] Advisory Commission on Intergovernmental Relations, *The Role of the States in Strengthening the Property Tax*, Vol. I, 1963, p. 14.

Central data processing at the state level, appropriately coordinated in the future with federal data processing systems devoted to handling relevant tax data and linked with satellite centers in basic assessment districts, offers the hope of adjusting *ad valorem* taxation to the needs of the future.[7]

The logic of administrative centralization appears strong. It does not necessarily require the delegation of tax rate decisions to the state. But if this logic is less than convincing to some, the least that can be said is that revitalization of the administrative status quo is desirable, if the traditional case for decentralization is to have more than symbolic meaning. On balance, the thrust of reform favors centralization of the assessment process.

Base and Rate Adjustments. Property tax reform possibilities include various adjustments in the definition of the tax base and the level of the rate applied to taxable property. Argument waxes and wanes; one man's base erosion is another man's scientific delimitation of appropriate taxability; agreement is by no means frequent or all inclusive. During any period of time, the property tax base expands and contracts like an accordion as men and the policies they create respond to differing needs and perceptions as well as to changing administrative capacity.

The nineteenth-century general property tax apparently or at least implicitly assumed that all property was sufficiently homogeneous so that it could be taxed *ad valorem* on a uniform basis. Subsequent property tax development—to be sure at different rates in different jurisdictions—has involved increased exemption or differential treatment of various property categories. The result is a heterogeneous pattern of exemption and differential taxation of quite heterogeneous types of property. I do not feel that all of this development fits under the convenient semantic label of base erosion. On the other hand, nor is our potential capacity of tax administration so limited as to justify the scope of some property tax exemptions. A liberal infusion of funds to ad-

[7] Model Property Tax Committee Report, 1964, p. 194.

ministrative budgets could, I suspect, dispel the mythology of administrative incapacity rather quickly.

Be that as it may, brief review of several somewhat oversimplified subsets of the conventional orthodoxy will lay a foundation for a glance at the future. It seems that there are several types of approaches to defining the tax base under the property tax. These alternative approaches merit brief discussion.

The "realty only" approach would limit *ad valorem* tax design to real estate and exempt other property categories from taxation. Of course, there is a difficulty in defining the boundary line between real property and personal property, but we may grant that somewhere there is a definition in a particular jurisdiction at that point in time. The "real and tangibles only" approach would exempt intangible personalty on the multiple grounds that representative property taxation is unjustified double taxation, that the yield of intangible property is taxed already as income under the income tax in many jurisdictions and by the federal government, and that experience indicates that intangible personal property taxation *ad valorem* is not administratively feasible. This argument, on both equity and expediency grounds, would conclude that intangible personalty should be exempt. Next, "the real and only some tangibles" approach. This excludes all intangibles and some tangible personal property. The exemption of tangible personal property would depend, of course, on the attitude, experience, and what side of the table the proponent was on. But conventionally exemptions would include household personalty, much agricultural personalty, and, with far less unanimity, business inventories, and, with still less agreement than that, tangible personal property used in business. This set of ideas reflects concern for administrative feasibility, differential tax burdens by property category, and to some extent the presumed marginal locational effect of business tax rates. Finally, there is "the almost all property" concept, the nineteenth-century idea from which the others have developed or evolved. It has not proved feasible, as we know, given our mixture of administrative capacity, will to administer, and general tax system.

Experience suggests that only the first three are reasonable options; and while it is clear that intangibles can be taxed effectively, it is unlikely that it will be often done. Cautious prediction suggests that the probable line of future development is toward the "real and only some tangibles" approach. If this or some similar concept becomes the emergent reality, base erosion remains a very real hazard. If the property tax is to remain productive or to regain lost productivity, base erosion needs to be avoided or offset.

Oddly enough, while these remarks appear applicable to property taxation as it exists in fact, several other observations are relevant. As the relative significance of types of property changes, one would suppose that the basic application of the property tax would change similarly. The simple case of the largely exempt personal passenger automobile illustrates the defective responsiveness of *ad valorem* taxation. The property tax has simply not responded to changes in the property institution.

Actually, the operation of American society in recent decades has created a wide variety of new forms of property and quasi-property which have not as yet been completely assimilated or delimited by our legal system. They have, of course, generated a scholarly literature because in an affluent society the rate of literature production exceeds that of society in assimilating ideas —which is as it should be. At any rate, we can say that the property tax has not moved by bold bounds as the institution of property itself has changed.

Rate adjustments have not been considered at length here. Legal or extralegal adjustments and differentials may be simple give-aways or rational classification devices designed to facilitate administration and/or stimulate development. In general, those in favor of tax rate differentials bear the burden of proof, and by no means do they always carry it well.

Alternative Ways of Taxing Property. The property tax is old enough and has been the subject of strident criticism long enough that a series of alternative ways of taxing property or property elements have been suggested by a rather substantial diversity of persons, both lay and professional. These are amply discussed in the literature and include (1) taxation of property on the basis of annual income, actual or hypothetical, rather than on a market value type assessment; (2) site value taxation with all the ideas that are associated with that notion; (3) levy upon land value increments; and (4) increased reliance upon user charges. Despite the varying attractiveness of these proposals, basic requirements of equity and revenue adequacy as well as the tradition of slow, deliberate, and glacial change in property tax patterns lead to the tentative conclusion that not much is to be expected soon by way of operational progress along these particular routes. If the short-term future proves this forecast in error, it will be less than surprising and by no means especially disappointing. However, at the moment a different outcome simply seems improbable.

Proposed Tax Substitutes. Repeatedly during the past eighty years, alternative taxes have been suggested as desirable, attractive, and, on occasion, even alluring replacements for *ad valorem* taxation of some or all property. Personal and corporate income levies, general sales taxes and congeries of selective excises, even in nontourist states, and, more recently, value added or income-produced taxes have all had more than one day in court. Many of these are attractive indeed because of some mixture of equity, neutrality, non-neutrality and/or revenue productivity. Today, they are largely pre-empted and are no longer obvious substitutes, particularly when psychological factors are taken into account. Nevertheless, whenever there is an effective consensus, such grand tax substitutions can be made. My only comment is that both recent history and instinct suggest the relative improbability of grand substitutional action. Rejection of this possibility is in terms of probabilities rather than merits—yet the very nature of federalism is pragmatic.

The history of the property tax confirms the inherent complexity of the assessment process. The difficulty of determining current and past values is exceeded only by the requirements of effective prediction. Error is easy, failure is by no means unique, and evasive action not altogether inappropriate.

As through a glass darkly, one may dimly perceive some few of the probable contours of the future. I see no short-term grand synthesis of received reform suggestions. Rather a continuation of present trends seems likely with inter-governmental transfer payments providing a useful mechanism which incidentally may take the heat off property tax reform urges. Time prevents discussion of the merits, desirability, or symmetry of this alternative, but it is noted as a probability. Moreover, continuation of this trend may widen the gap between locally administered, traditional property taxes and the requirements and opportunities of tomorrow. The least that can usefully be done, in my opinion, is to revitalize the administration of the property tax along the lines suggested in the Bird Report. To do less is to vote for both additional public sector centralization and the adoption or expansion of other forms of taxation. As Netzer well said, "It is in the nature of life to present societies and individuals with hard choices." [8]

It seems clear that property tax reform is still one option open to state and local governments as they adjust to changing circumstances. Inertia is another option—which will not serve very well. The substance, if not the semantics, of property tax reform should be advanced on the agenda of governmental decision-making. *Natura non facit saltum* has long applied to the property tax—it may indeed continue to do so. If such is the case, a not insignificant opportunity will have been foregone.

[8] Dick Netzer, *Economics of the Property Tax* (Washington: The Brookings Institution, 1966), 220.

PROPERTY TAX PROBLEMS CONFRONTING STATE AND LOCAL GOVERNMENTS

Arthur P. Becker

IT IS GOOD to reflect periodically on any habit, custom, or law that has been followed for many years to determine its condition, relevance, and place in our present society. Accordingly, it is good to examine the property tax, which had its inception in Colonial days and is now entering the last third of the twentieth century as the primary source of local tax revenue in the United States. We will look at the tax in historical perspective and try to identify some of the major problems that it faces today and evaluate their substance in terms of accepted standards of taxation and the characteristics, needs, and problems of our changing society.

It should first be pointed out that the property tax is waging a defensive battle. The overall fiscal role of the property tax has been diminished in the United States since the latter part of the nineteenth century by means of a procession of exemptions that have seriously eroded the tax base; at the same time other taxes have been enacted to provide additional revenues. Even though the tax remains on the defensive, it continues to provide a large portion of local tax revenue. In 1965 it yielded $22.9 billion— approximately 88 per cent of local tax revenues. Moreover, the tax per capita has risen from $3 in 1860 to $117.79 in 1965. It is interesting to note that the tax represented 3.4 per cent of the gross national product from 1870 to 1880 and an equal amount in 1962–63.[1] These statistics suggest that while the tax has not grown in relative importance since 1870, it has in the aggregate not declined. This may be regarded as a remarkable accomplishment, considering the criticism which the tax has evoked.

Criticism of the property tax in the United States is unmatched

---

[1] Dick Netzer, *Economics of the Property Tax* (Washington, D.C.: The Brookings Institution, 1966), 2.

in scholarly literature. However, one should not evaluate a tax in terms of the amount of criticism it receives; criticism is often misleading. In the case of the property tax, criticism has become a part of our folklore—strictures long ago inspired by a particular weakness of the property tax retain their currency, even after the weakness has been removed. For example, Professor E. R. A. Seligman's denunciation of the general property tax in 1895 is quoted repeatedly,[2] though his indictment was primarily directed toward the taxation of intangibles and the unprofessional nature of the administration. Most states have exempted intangibles from the property tax, and many tax jurisdictions have attained excellent professional standards.

Even after putting criticism of the property tax in perspective, enough remnants remain to justify the view that the tax is afflicted with important ailments. One of the major problems that has confronted the property tax since its inception is lack of administrative effectiveness. Despite considerable progress that has been made in many of our major cities, the quality of property tax administration remains inexcusably low and entirely unwarranted. The standards of administration remain by and large far below accepted standards for other major taxes, such as income and sales taxes. The reason is quite clear—the property tax has remained the responsibility of the lowest levels of government, which all too often cannot support good administration and cannot easily attract professional workers. Income and sales taxes, however, are administered by the federal and state governments, which have far greater ability to attract competent personnel and to finance adequately the administration of their taxes.

Quality of Assessment

Some problems of assessment are as acute as ever. One is the infrequency of assessments. Any delay in reassessing property usually produces inequities, especially when accompanied with

[2] Edwin R. A. Seligman, *Essays in Taxation* (New York: Macmillan and Co., 1895), 59–61.

rapid price rises, a phenomenon which we have experienced in considerable measure since World War II. The longer the reassessment is put off, the greater the inequities become; meanwhile, more persons develop a vested interest in delaying reassessment still longer. The major inequalities of assessments within a given district are found (1) between classes of property, both functional (residential, commercial, industrial) and physical (land, improvements, tangibles, and intangibles); (2) internally between high property values and low value properties; and (3) between similar properties in the same class.

Both infrequency and inequity of assessments within a given district customarily arise when the district has insufficient financial resources, that is, if its property tax base is too small, to maintain a large enough and fully qualified professional staff of assessors. The question legitimately rises as to whether property tax administration should not be turned over to a larger jurisdiction of one or more counties.

Another type of assessment inequality is that which persists among districts which contribute to a higher level of government —the county or the state. The reasons for this type of inequity are two: (1) the general practice of assessing property at a fractional ratio of its full value and (2) the existence of assessment jurisdictions smaller than the largest governmental unit which depends heavily upon the property tax, namely the county. The standard solution to this problem has been the practice of central assessment and equalization.

Today, however, after more than a hundred years of fractional assessments and permitted inequalities in assessments, the courts have dropped, figuratively, a nuclear bomb on these disreputable practices. It began with a 1957 decision by the New Jersey Supreme Court which required that the local tax assessor assess all taxable real property within his district at 100 per cent of value, and not at a fraction of such value.[3] Similar decisions have been

---

[3] Smitz v. Township of Middletown, 23 N.J. 580, 130A 2d 15 (1957).

rendered by the Florida Supreme Court,[4] the Kentucky Court of Appeals,[5] the Federal District Court of Middle Tennessee,[6] and the Chancery Court of Davidson County, Tennessee;[7] and it appears that this trend will expand to a number of other states. Probably no other state constitutional requirement has been violated so widely as the full value assessment provision. If this violation is destined finally to come to an end, it will not have happened too soon. Full value assessment has hitherto been regarded as an unattainable ideal among assessors. And, corollarially, removing the problem of underassessment will sweep away the problems of unequal assessment.

The sudden judicial support has caught most property tax assessors by surprise, and many have responded with disbelief and uncertainty as to how to implement the decision. Some states are worried that 100 per cent assessment will catch up with them, and they are preparing to constitutionalize uniform fractional assessment ratios. These moves seem to be ill-advised for two reasons. No matter what fractional assessment ratio is chosen as the constitutional standard, it too will become obsolete as assessment ratios decrease with the passage of time. Secondly, it has been found that uniformity in assessment is greater where assessment ratios are higher. With low assessment ratios a small error in assessment would lead to a magnified inequality. As an illustration, a variation of 1 percentage point from a 10 per cent assessment ratio would be ten times as great as a 1 percentage point deviation from a 100 per cent assessment ratio.

It is a universal complaint that property tax burdens have reached an intolerable level. Yet this is hardly supported by the facts as found among local governments in most states. As we have already seen, the property tax today is no greater a percentage

---

[4] Walter v. Schuler, 176 So. 2d 81.
[5] Russman v. Lockett, CCH Ky. Tax Rep pp. 200–766.
[6] Louisville and Nashville Railway v. State Board of Equalization, 249F. Supp. 894 (1966).
[7] Southern Railway Co. v. State Board of Equalization, Davidson County Chancery Court, II, Book 77, (1966), 191.

of the gross national product than it was in 1870–80. It is also true that the percentage of income paid in property taxes in some forty states is substantially below the percentage in the ten states that use the property tax most heavily.

The heavy burden ascribed to the property tax is due not so much to the absolute dollar burden, or even to the relative burden in terms of income, as it is to the failure to provide an easier and more convenient means of payment. None of the other major taxes have this defect. The sales tax by its very nature provides for a small payment every time a purchase is made. The income tax once suffered the same defect as the property tax does today until tax payments were deducted from weekly or monthly earnings, thereby placing the tax on a pay-as-you-go basis. The same formula could be applied with very little difficulty to the property tax. There is no reason why the property owner cannot have a portion of his tax on his home withheld from his earnings as is done with federal and state income taxes.

While it is not the purpose of this paper to make specific suggestions for the fundamental reform of the property tax payment system, it is suggested that one avenue of improvement might begin with an act of Congress, offering the use of the tax withholding machinery of the Internal Revenue Service to any property tax administration district consisting of one or more counties, with minimum standards of population and real property in terms of full value. Minimum functions of an eligible district should be those of listing and assessing realty, and billing and collecting the tax. The federal government might even offer a small financial inducement, such as absorbing a portion of the expenses of the property tax administrative district.

The homeowner would have a pro-rated portion of his total annual real estate tax withheld from each of his paychecks and forwarded from the district revenue office to the property tax administrative district in which the taxpayer lives. This district would then distribute the appropriate portions of the tax to the local governments within its jurisdiction. Owners of small holdings of income property might be given the option of having their property taxes withheld from their earnings. Holders of large income properties would forward portions of the property tax in the same manner as employers do today on income tax withheld. There are many interesting aspects of this proposal, and they require further exploration. There do not seem to be, however, any insuperable obstacles to placing the property tax on a modern pay-as-you-go plan, which is necessary if the tax is to play a major role in financing government in the future.

Erosion of the Tax Base

Another major property tax problem facing local governments is the relentless erosion of the tax base. This erosion is the byproduct of a wide variety of exemptions given by constitutional privilege or legislation over the years. The magnitude and growth of these exemptions have developed to significant proportions both for realty and personalty.

Real estate has traditionally been exempt from property taxes if it was owned by domestic governments and their agencies, educational institutions, religious organizations, or philanthropic and fraternal associations. The public or semi-public purposes to which this property is dedicated have been given as a justification for these exemptions. One can easily show, however, that carelessness in preparing property rolls has frequently conferred tax exempt status on property that qualifies nominally more than substantively. There are also a growing number of communities that serve tax exempt facilities that bear a relatively high proportion of total assessed realty. Communities whose primary economic activities revolve around government or higher education find themselves in this tight situation. The traditional exemptions of realty have been so expanded that a new plane of vastly different dimensions exists. Within this situation is found the highly profitable business property which is accorded tax exempt status when acquired by educational, religious, and philanthropic associations.

Besides the expansion of traditional types of realty exemptions, a whole new series of exemptions has arisen and provoked serious controversy. Among these are exemptions for homesteads, veterans, aged persons, unfortunate persons, housing, urban redevelopment projects, industry, and agriculture. These new types probably began with homestead exemptions granted to alleviate hardship for homeowners during the Depression. Some eleven states provide this kind of exemption today. Economists have generally regarded the homestead exemption as unfair and undesirable. The Advisory Commission on Intergovernmental Relations states:

> The policy of homestead exemption involves a substantial amount of injustice. It starts out by awarding a special bonus to one class of property in the form of an increase in its capital value and then provides a continuing subsidy to this class at the expense of the tenant and business classes. Rented properties occupied by low income families help to pay the taxes from which homeowners—all homeowners, not just small homeowners—are freed, and business interests suffer hardship unless they are able to shift the tax increases to their customers and clients.
>
> Since all of the States assess property at some fraction of full value, moreover, the value of homestead exemption is much greater than the law appears to indicate. . . .[8]

In one fourth of the states we find exemptions offered for one or more categories of unfortunate persons. The circumstances necessary to produce eligibility for this type of exemption include deafness and insanity in Alabama, Hansen's disease in Hawaii, blindness in Alabama, Indiana, New Hampshire, Rhode Island, and Utah, and widowhood in Florida and Utah. Exemption for the aged seems to be the very latest effort to make the property tax conform to the ability to pay principle. Massachusetts, Indiana, New Jersey, and Oregon have adopted variations of real estate exemptions for the aged. The policy of assisting unfortunates and

[8] Advisory Commission on Intergovernmental Relations, *The Role of the States in Strengthening the Property Tax*, prepared by Frederick L. Bird and Edna T. Bird (Washington, 1963), Vol. I, 79.

the aged by means of property tax exemptions, while honorably motivated, is of relatively little help in its partial approach to the problems of these people. The achievement of ability to pay by means of exemptions cannot be applied to the real estate property tax without seriously weakening it in terms of equity, yield, and economic productivity.

Redistribution of income by means of the property tax is an uncertain and risky business. This problem is exemplified in the position expressed by the Twentieth Century Fund: "The use of property tax exemptions for redistributing the burden is hindered by the difficulty of knowing where the burden lies and where it will lie after the change is made. Although this difficulty is common to all taxes, it is especially important for the property tax because of the size and universality of the burden." [9] A redistribution of income for persons paying property and sales taxes could be better achieved by means of supplementary income payments. Moreover, considering the financial resources of various levels of government, the responsibility for income distribution cannot be assumed by local governments because the attempt would erode their limited and sole source of tax revenues. This responsibility can more fairly and realistically be assumed by the state and federal governments, a fact that is generally recognized by experts in the field of government finance.

Property tax exemptions of some kind to veterans are found in thirty-two states. Appreciation, gratitude, and assistance to the veteran are worthy motives and may well justify a continuing bonus or disability payment. It is entirely wrong, however, for local governments to assume this financial responsibility and effect it by means of property tax exemptions. Veterans' benefits should not be contingent upon property ownership; the less affluent, property-less veteran gets nothing. Also, veterans' exemptions, like homestead exemptions, are capricious, tend toward underassessment to stay within ceilings, produce many administrative complications, and exhibit many of the other

[9] Twentieth Century Fund, Inc., *Facing the Tax Problems*, 1937, p. 296.

undesirable effects of homestead exemptions. From the stand-point of financial resources as well as jurisdiction over defense matters, it is properly the function of the federal government to provide for veterans' benefits. In the absence of federal action, a state program based upon need or merit would be far better than the present exemptions.

Among the newer style exemptions are those granted to in-dustry as a result of the competition among states to attract in-dustrial plants. Although many states have granted such exemptions in the past, only eight, primarily in New England and in the South, now offer limited term property tax exemptions to new industrial plants today. This has promoted interstate tax warfare and has interfered with the development of a fair prop-erty tax system. Industrial property tax exemptions often turn out to be costly and disappointing to local communities and im-pose a hardship on taxpayers beyond what can be reasonably justified. Moreover, either in or out of the state, these exemptions damage the tax base of communities which lose industrial firms. It should also be noted that a substantial industry is not ordinarily interested in a community which offers it a short-term handout in exchange for an unbalanced and inequitable tax structure be-cause, after its years of cut-rate property taxes end, the industry itself will be forced to shoulder the extra burden of luring still another industry to the same community.

The crisis facing urban America involving housing and renewal of the decaying portions of our cities has led New York, New Jersey, Massachusetts, Missouri and Wisconsin to grant certain property tax exemptions. These states believe that their urban redevelopment projects have been hampered by the property tax, and it was hoped that property tax concessions or abatements would stimulate socially desired redevelopment. No other type of exemption has raised a greater storm of opposition. The con-troversy is reflected in a recent Wisconsin state supreme court decision which declared unconstitutional that state's "tax assess-ment freeze." This does not mean, however, that we may not expect to witness attempts by other states to modify the real estate tax system in an effort to create incentive and stimulate the rebuilding and remodeling of decaying real property.

No discussion of property tax exemptions is complete without reference to the personal property tax. Historically, no component of the property tax has received more condemnation. This criticism arose so early that personal property assessments began to decline as a share of total assessed value about one hundred years ago, even though the growth in value of intangibles has been more rapid than that of real assets. Today the assessed value of personal property is only 17 per cent of total assessments throughout the nation.[10] This has come about as a result of legal and illegal exemptions.

Intangible personal property has been exempted from the local tax in all but nine states, although intangibles are still taxed, in a special category, in twenty states. Taxing intangibles is really important only in West Virginia. The general exemption is due to two factors: (1) taxing intangibles is generally regarded as "double taxation" and (2) intangibles are too easily concealed.

Five states (Delaware, Hawaii, New Jersey, New York, and Pennsylvania) exempt tangible personal property completely. Twenty-nine states exempt most non-business personalty, *i.e.*, household effects, either entirely or partially. Nineteen states exempt motor vehicles completely. An important issue today in many states is whether non-business and even business tangible property should be exempted completely.

Major arguments against taxing tangible personal property are based upon the following:

(1) The difficulty of discovering tangibles simply in order to construct the tax rolls.

(2) Inequity of assessment as of a given date.

(3) Difficulties in determining value.

10 Netzer, *Economics of the Property Tax*, 139.

(4) Disproportionately high administrative expenses, due to the necessity of field audits.

(5) The fact that the tax falls most heavily on the low turnover type of business which requires substantial fixed assets and inventories, while businesses with a high turnover, few assets, and small inventories go largely untaxed, even though they may be productive of great wealth.

(6) The disproportionate share of the levy the large taxpayer pays while the small taxpayer tends to pay less than his share or escape the levy entirely. Such discrimination is explained by the fact that the large taxpayer keeps accurate records, assessors are more zealous in checking the accounts of large taxpayers, and small taxpayers without records tend to give the assessor a very low value. This is known as "taxation by consent," and may very well involve evasion.

(7) The heavy, often unfair, burden the tax imposes on businesses, especially those facing interstate competition from firms enjoying exemptions in their own states.

The above arguments are powerful enough to justify the summary elimination of household effects as a basis of taxation. The arguments do not, however, apply to motor vehicles, which are uniquely taxable both administratively and because of their enormous social cost, which seems to exceed the present taxes on them (for licenses and fuel) by far.

An Evaluation of the Property Tax Problem

In an effort to understand and evaluate property tax problems and to help decide upon policy recommendations, it may be useful to compare the four basic components of the tax in terms of standard tax objectives. This type of analysis is, of course, largely judgmental and oversimplified, but it is helpful nevertheless in summarizing and explaining what is behind the trend today. To illustrate, Table 1 sets forth the different components of property, and a score of ten, five, or zero is assigned according to whatever evaluation is made in terms of standard tax objectives. Neutrality in economic effect is assigned a maximum of 20 points, which actually may be weighed too lightly in view of the fact that equity carries 40 points (items 1, 2, 3, and 4) and administration 20 points (items 5 and 6). Out of a maximum score of 100 the author assigned 100 to land, 65 to improvements, 45 to tangible personalty, and only 20 to intangible personalty. Other evaluations

TABLE 1

ANALYSIS OF PROPERTY TAX COMPONENTS
IN TERMS OF STANDARD TAX OBJECTIVES

	Land	Improvements	Tangible Personalty	Intangible Personalty
1. Accords with Benefits Received	10	10	5	0
2. Accords with Ability to Pay	10	10	10	10
3. Accords with Natural Rights	10	0	0	0
4. Adequate and Dependable	10	10	5	0
5. Simple to Understand	10	10	10	5
6. Ease of Listing Determining Tax Base	10	10	5	0
7. Ease of Determining Value of Tax Base	10	5	5	5
8. Ease of Applying Uniform Treatment	10	10	5	0
9. Neutral Economic Effect	20	0	0	0
Total Score (out of 100 possible)	100	65	45	20

may yield different totals, but the relative positions of the components would probably not change. It is not difficult to see why taxing intangibles has fallen into such disrepute and why it is followed closely by most tangible personalty.

The standards of taxation that are demanded today are higher than those of yesterday, but they are not determined by what is being taxed. If quality administration were applied to the property tax with the same vigor as it is to the income tax, the most important components, namely land and improvements, would compare rather well. With few exceptions, taxes on personal property would not.

Another serious problem that our analysis of the property tax reveals is the poor showing of all components except land in terms of the economic effect of the tax. The tax on land values alone is neutral, whereas the tax on both improvements and personalty exerts an inhibiting effect on production. Perhaps a partial understanding of this latter has led to the legislation to exempt agricultural property, industry, housing, and urban redevelopment from at least part of the property tax and/or for a limited period of time. However, all of these efforts at tax abatement treat property components alike, an indiscriminate policy that cannot be supported by our analysis.

Because taxing improvements and personalty interferes with and inhibits new construction, remodeling, and other productive activities, any property tax abatements should be directed toward these components, by means of exemptions, and not toward land. Moreover, taxing land values more heavily could make up the loss in yield arising from the tax abatement in improvements and personalty without any detrimental economic effect, because taxes on land are neutral. Apparently, policy makers have little awareness or an inadequate understanding of the different economic effects of taxing land versus improvements and personalty.

Conclusion

In conclusion we may highlight those property tax problems which have become most pressing in our time. Administratively, they relate to the need for professionalizing the practice of assessing and putting the tax on a pay-as-you-go basis. Putting the property tax on a pay-as-you-go basis is feasible and long overdue.

Substantively, the most urgent problems are these: First, we must stop the continued erosion of the property tax base—the partial or complete exemption of additional kinds of real estate tax—and even restore many exempted properties which do not meet reasonable tests for exemption. Some churches are beginning to realize this and to recognize that the overall benefits would outweigh whatever disadvantages might come to various congregations in having to raise extra funds here. Alternative methods can and should be devised to achieve the hoped for objectives that have motivated real estate property tax exemptions. Secondly, we must modify the tax in such a way that it possesses a greater degree of economic neutrality. Stated positively, this means that the tax should be changed so as to remove inhibitions and provide maximum incentive to put land to its highest and best use. If these problems are treated properly, the property tax will play a constructive role in future tax policy.

RECENT DEVELOPMENTS IN PROPERTY TAXATION IN FLORIDA: *A Case Study*

C. H. DONOVAN

UNTIL THE 1920's Florida, like most other states, depended heavily on the property tax for state as well as local government revenues. The advent of the automobile user taxes, the adoption of taxes on corporate franchises and of specific business levies to accompany the traditional business license taxes, to-together with special taxes on racing and alcoholic beverages in the thirties were the only other major steps taken to supplement the state's receipts from property taxes prior to World War II. The dramatic growth of Florida during the past half-century, and especially since World War II, is a story known to all. From a position at the bottom of the southern states in population and income, the state has risen to the top of both indices. Although per capita income is well below the national average, the state now ranks as the ninth most populous in the Union. During one period of accelerated growth, 1890 to 1920, Florida's population more than doubled; by the time we entered World War II, the state had more than five times as many people as it had had in 1890. Income, in the five years from 1920 to 1925, increased by 100 per cent; but half of this gain was lost in the next five years, when recession hit the state's economy well before the nationwide Depression.

Property Tax Changes, 1920–40

The collapse of the Florida land boom in 1926 ushered in a period of rapidly declining land values and tax receipts. This is reflected in the total of assessed valuations (Table 2) for property tax purposes. Property assessments increased from less than $100 million at the turn of the century to a 1926 peak of $786 million, total assessed valuation. In the next six years nearly half of this, $350 million, disappeared from the tax rolls. Recovery was slight during the depressed thirties. As late as 1940, the total was some $260 million below the 1926 figure. The steep decline in assessed valuations was accompanied by a sharp increase in tax delinquencies. For example, in 1930 more than one quarter of the acreage in Florida was sold to the state for taxes. This trend is further indicated by a decline in the percentage of state taxes collected by the county tax collectors. Collected for the fiscal years 1932 and 1933 were 79 and 52.8 per cent, respectively.

TABLE 2

TRENDS IN POPULATION, INCOME, AND PROPERTY TAXES
IN FLORIDA, 1920–65

	Population (Thousands)	Personal Income (Millions$)	Per Capita Income	Assessed Valuation (Millions$)	Property Taxes (Millions$)	Total Taxes (Millions$)
1920	968	412	460	410		
1925	1,264	917	725	621		
1930	1,468	671	457	576		
					25*	70*
1940	1,897	982	518	526		
1941	2,058	1,211	588	2,127	55	124
1945	2,420	2,895	1,196	2,598		
1950	2,771	3,632	1,293	4,244		
1955	3,670	6,088	1,659	6,945	209	523
1960	4,951	9,843	1,969	14,790	342	920
1964	5,650	12,841	2,251	23,994	481	1,258
1965	5,805	14,041	2,423	29,760	507	1,353

Sources: U. S. Bureau of Census
U. S. Department of Commerce
Report of the Comptroller of the State of Florida
*Data for "Property Taxes" and "Total Taxes" are for 1932.

This situation resulted in heavy public pressure for property tax relief. Each session of the legislature from 1929 to 1937 produced one or more bills which permitted the delinquent taxpayer to compromise his taxes. Although no comprehensive study of the effect of this legislation has been made, scattered evidence indicates that only a very small fraction of the delinquent taxes were ever paid. Aside from personal and economic hardship, one of the chief arguments used to support this legislation was that it would restore the properties to the tax rolls and create a tax climate that would encourage owners (new or old) to improve their property. This in turn would encourage economic progress.

Two constitutional amendments, adopted in the late twenties (1928) and early thirties (1934), were designed to correct the property tax problem. Both of these amendments limited the scope of the property tax and thereby contributed to its decline in relative importance as a source of governmental revenue. The first amendment provided for the exemption of a wide variety of industrial establishments from *ad valorem* taxes. The amendment included all industrial plants which should be established after July 29 that were engaged in the manufacture of steel vessels, automobile tires, fabrics and textiles, wood pulp, paper, fiber board, automobiles, automobile parts, aircraft, aircraft parts, glass and pottery, or the refining of sugar and oil. Motion pictures production was added by amendment. Thus, Florida became one of the first states to supplement whatever basic economic and social attractions it might offer new industry by extending tax exemptions.

Only one of the exempt industries became a problem—the paper pulp industry which was encouraged to establish major plants in the state during the lifetime of this amendment. Refinements of the process for converting pulp from pine trees were probably more important than tax exemption as far as the location of those mills was concerned.

The exemption of the manufacture of steel vessels from property tax had an interesting kickback. This was generally interpreted as ship building, but a number of tin can companies claimed exemption under the amendment. This posed the question of what is a tin can? Ultimately it was defined as a steel vessel; hence these plants were exempt from property taxes as specified in the legislation of 1928.

More pervasive in its effects on property tax administration and yields was the homestead exemption adopted in 1934. The presence of widespread tax delinquency and forced tax sales caused the legislature to enact an unusual and liberal homestead act. This homestead amendment as adopted in 1934 and changed in 1963 is:

> Exemption of homestead from taxation.—Every person who has the legal title or beneficial title in equity to real property in this state and who resides thereon and in good faith makes the same his or her permanent home, or the permanent home of another or others legally or naturally dependent upon said person, shall be entitled to an exemption from all taxation, except for assessments for special benefits, up to the assessed valuation of five thousand dollars on said home and contiguous real property, as defined in Article X, Section 1, of the Constitution, for the year 1939 and thereafter
>
> . . . .
>
> provided that in Sarasota County the first two thousand dollars of the assessed valuation of such property shall be taxable for school purposes only and the exemption shall apply to the next five thousand dollars for school purposes only of assessed valuation.

The exemption of the first $5,000 of the assessed value gave rise to pressure on assessing officials to assess property at less than full market value. The absence of effective state supervision, or any statewide equalization machinery, fostered this practice. As a result one fourth to one third of the property in the state went off the tax rolls. The tax load on rental property and commercial and industrial properties not covered by the new industry exemption grew disproportionately.

In 1940 another constitutional amendment abolishing all state taxes on real and tangible personal property was enacted. This heightened the feeling that the state should have no concern about local property tax administration. However, in the 1941 legislative session, Governor Spessard L. Holland put through his program for a roll back of millage rates in return for the adoption of full value assessments. This dramatically quadrupled assessed valuations (see Table 2), but World War II tended to offset the effects of this program.

51

Postwar Steps to Relieve the Burden on Property Taxes

Several events took place during the forties that seemed to ease the load on property taxes. As mentioned above, the state relinquished this tax, except for intangibles, to the local units in 1940. In 1948, the constitutional exemption for certain types of industries was allowed to expire without any concerted attempt at renewal. This gave several rural counties a big boost in their tax base.

The early war years produced a change in distribution formula of the state gasoline and racing taxes which gave the thinly populated counties a disproportionate share of the revenue from these taxes. In fact, each of the sixty-seven counties shared equally in one half of the racing taxes distributed to counties. Area and mileage were the major criteria used in the distribution of approximately 50 per cent of the gasoline tax among the counties. In 1949, the state recognized the financial pinch on the rapidly growing urban centers and shared the increased state cigarette tax with the cities where it was collected. All of these measures eased, for a time, pressure on the property taxpayer.

The most far-reaching development was the Minimum Foundation Program for public schools. Adopted in 1947 and extended by subsequent legislatures to include state junior colleges, this program committed the state to a broad grant-in-aid program for schools. It was recognized that some measure of local ability to raise funds was needed. A cumbersome, weighted formula was devised, using sales tax returns, value of farm products, state assessed railroad and telegraph property, automobile licenses, and gainfully employed workers—data all available on a county basis. It may be pointed out that this was the basis of the choice of what went into the formula—figures available on a statewide as well as a county basis could provide a useful formula for all levels of government.

During the past twenty years, state aid for public schools has increased from a modest $40 million to nearly $300 million annually. Until the recent advent of federal aid on a broad scale, state funds furnished more than half of the public school support. Demand on local (*i.e.*, property tax) resources has grown rapidly as well. The constitutional millage limitation of ten mills for operating purposes and requirements for referenda to implement the millage limit have created pressures which have given rise to a higher level of assessments. Inequities among different types and values of property have been intensified by the homestead exemption.

Assessment Ratio Struggle

For some twenty years following the constitutional amendment requiring that "the legislature shall provide for a uniform and equal rate of taxation," fractional assessment was accepted with no effective attempt by the state toward equalization. In the mid-thirties railroads, the only property not locally assessed, sued to get their assessments lowered to the levels set by county assessors. Various studies showed wide variations from county to county: some property was assessed at less than 5 per cent of true value, while other property was assessed at more than 65 per cent. When the state surrendered the power to tax real property, there was less incentive for equalization. Governor Holland did, however, succeed in getting acceptance of the principle of full value assessment in return for legislation requiring a roll back of the millage.

The drive for equal assessment was not resumed until the pressure of mounting school costs gave rise to reform demands in the mid-fifties. Governor Leroy Collins attempted to use the authority of his office to persuade county assessors to implement full value assessments. Those counties complying with the request argued that the state should bring the level of assessment on railroad and telegraph property up to the same 100 per cent level. The railroads responded with an argument that produced a compromise assessment on railroad properties varied according to the level of locally assessed property. It is interesting to note that the Railroad Assessment Board, an ex-officio three-man segment of the elective cabinet, determined the level of local assessments. In 1964, based upon the figures furnished by this agency, five counties were reported as assessing at 100 per cent of full value and one at a low of 27.4 per cent.

The legislature made several attempts to define what full value meant for assessment purposes and to establish criteria to guide local assessors. An act was passed which required that land, even inside city limits, being used for agricultural purposes was to be assessed on an acreage basis in line with its value as agricultural land. The cultivation of a few citrus trees on acreage within city limits or in the adjacent suburbs could qualify property for this agricultural zoning tax exemption. This requirement seemed to be contrary to the uniformity clause of the constitution. The Florida Supreme Court, however, upheld the act; the decision was 4 to 3.

Following this decision, several cases concerning assessment ratio were brought to the courts. One of the first involved Dade County (Miami), the state's largest county. A circuit court decision in 1964, upheld by the Florida Supreme Court, required that all property be assessed at full value. The impact of this decision on other counties is reflected in the taxpayers' suit against the assessor of Duval County (Jacksonville) requesting assessment of all property at its full value. The circuit court issued a landmark decision in favor of the taxpayers. An appeal of this decision to the Florida Supreme Court resulted in an opinion making the order apply to all counties in the state.

Tax rolls for 1965 began to reflect the effects of this decision (see Table 2). By 1968 the total value of all property in the state will probably exceed $45 billion, and slightly more than 20 per cent of this will be exempt from *ad valorem* taxes. This dramatic increase in assessed valuation has provoked widespread demands for *ad valorem* tax relief. A 1965 law gives the owner of property who feels his assessment is too high the right to demand that the property be put up for sale by the assessor. If the highest bid is lower than the assessed value, that figure must be accepted by the assessor. If, on the other hand, the bids exceed the assessed value, the property is then sold to the high bidder. Limited experience suggests that property owners are reluctant to challenge the assessor's valuation of their property.

Recent Governmental Changes

Before examining some of the property tax prospects in Florida, a brief look at a few of the structural changes at the state and local government levels is in order. The three major changes are constitutional revision, reapportionment, and local government reform.

Since the adoption of the constitution in 1885 there have been hundreds of amendments proposed and dozens adopted. Some of these amendments prohibit income taxes and death taxes above the federal credit. The 1965 legislature authorized the establishment of a constitutional revision commission with broad representation. A draft of a new constitution prepared by this commission incorporates extensive revisions. The taxation and finance articles, although modified, retained most of the prohibitions mentioned above. The provision requiring uniform and equal rates of taxation was changed to permit classification of property according to type. Another provision permits local option to lower, or even eliminate, the homestead exemption.

On January 9, 1967, the legislature was convened in special session to consider the proposed new constitution. The United States Supreme Court handed down a decision declaring the apportionment formula on which the legislature was elected invalid. The federal district court to which the Supreme Court remanded the apportionment question took matters into its own hands and redistricted the state along county lines, producing less than 5 per cent deviation in population among the resulting districts. New elections were ordered and held from February 28 to March 28, with the legislature convening on schedule a week later; and between February 28 and March 28, three statewide elections were conducted. Many of the legislators elected in November chose not to run, or failed in re-election bids. The new legislature consists of seventy-nine new members in the House of Representatives and twelve new senators. The consequences for tax revision are uncertain at this juncture, but a revision of the formula for sharing state gasoline and racing taxes to give more to the populous counties seems assured of passage. The impact on local property taxes may be severe, if no replacement revenues are forthcoming from the state.

Consolidation of local governments, both inter-city and city-county, has been discussed for many years. After plans for more thorough integration of municipal governments with the county were rejected by the voters in Dade and other metropolitan counties, a metro charter was adopted for that county in 1957. It should be recalled that this was a landmark change in local government organization. The new governing body has assumed many of the functions formerly performed by the county or its nearly thirty municipalities. One of the provisions in its charter precipitated the first court decision ordering full value assessment. Currently, study commissions are at work in at least six more of the state's metropolitan counties looking toward some measure of city-county consolidation of function. Hopes for success are high even though legislative action and local voter approval must be obtained.

Over the past twenty years amendments to the state constitution have been adopted consolidating the tax assessing and tax collection functions for all units of government in each of six counties in a single assessment and a single collection office at the county level. The results have been well accepted. Initially there was some grumbling, but as time has passed the residents and local officials in these counties have become quite pleased. With the advent of full value assessment it seems likely that similar action will be taken for all counties. The Commission on State Tax Reform has so recommended.

A far bolder proposal to consolidate counties has been put before the current legislature by one of the county leaders. It would reduce the number of counties from sixty-seven to fifty by consolidating adjacent counties in seventeen of the more thinly populated areas of the state. Since several of the counties to be

56

eliminated do not raise enough local revenue to meet their pay-rolls, the sponsors feel that the result would lessen the overhead cost of government, not only for local property taxpayers but also for the state. While the proposal is by no means assured of adoption, the fact that it has been offered shows dramatically the meaning of reapportionment. If property tax relief is a firm goal, overhauling governmental structure to permit more efficient operation should not be overlooked.

In the property tax field several measures are now pending before the regular biennial session of the legislature. Many members of both houses and the governor have promised to do something for "the over-burdened property taxpayer." Putting a limit on millage rates for all taxing units, strengthening the roll-back provisions of existing laws, and even freezing current property taxes have been suggested. Various other proposals to turn back to the counties a share of increased state sales or excise taxes in exchange for a reduction of local property taxes have been stalled by uncertainty about the governor's no new tax pledge.

Liberalization of the homestead exemption has also been proposed. A flat increase, even doubling the present $5,000 exemption has been mentioned. Other proposals would double the exemption for homeowners over 65 years of age, or possibly even lower the age to 60, who are residents of the state prior to a future cut-off date and can demonstrate that they have less than a specified income. The rationale of this argument stems from the fact that many older people living on limited retirement incomes settled in Florida under the promise that their modest homes would be practically tax exempt under fractional assessment. Full value assessment has changed this outlook drastically.

All of these proposals for property tax relief are being made without much study of the actual burden of such taxes. In 1964–65 property tax collections per capita in Florida were $87.28, placing Florida thirty-third from top among the fifty states and far below the national average of $116.52. Unless we make the questionable assumption that in Florida we get more for our tax dollar because of better public management, more productive public servants, or an overworked climate, we must expect the performance of our governmental functions to be below the average for all states.

When we relate taxes to income, we find that Florida's state and local taxes amounted to $105.33 per $1,000 of personal income, slightly higher than the national average of $104.36. Florida ranked twenty-fifth in this respect. Property tax collections per $1,000 of personal income in Florida were $39.45, well below the national average of $45.99. Here Florida ranked thirtieth, but well above the other southern states. This aspect of interstate competition is the source of one of the pressures to limit *ad valorem* taxes in Florida.

How does Florida's tax system compare to the time-honored criteria of equity, economic effects, administrative efficiency, and fiscal productivity? The last part of the question is easiest to answer. With the biennial session of the legislature a month old this week, it appears that close to $100,000,000 a year in "new money" must be raised to adequately finance Florida's schools, universities, welfare, health, and other functions dependent on the General Revenue Fund. It seems unlikely that any such amounts can be made up from improved methods of government operation, or from the fruits of economic growth in the next two years.

We do not have an adequate basis for judging the fairness of Florida's tax system, though many have spoken on this. No adequate study has been made, for instance, to measure the amount of state and local taxes borne by a $100-a-week wage earner in Florida as compared to a $50,000-a-year executive. There is reason to believe the proportion of the former's income taken in taxes is greater. Would a family of four with an income of $5,000, $6,000, or $10,000 a year pay more in taxes if the sales tax were broadened to include food purchases or if the present tax were made four per cent, than they would if the same amount of money were raised from increased property taxes with full value assessment and elimination of the present homestead exemption? All of these are potential alternatives. Maybe not realistic political alternatives but they are potential alternatives. Nor do we have adequate information on the effect of our tax system, or proposed changes, on the growth of our state. Various groups are quick to point out the impact on their special interests.

The tax structure as a whole has been castigated as a hodge-podge of confusion and inequities, and this is almost a direct quote from any number of political campaign speeches. Many of these criticisms are unfounded. Over the years the Florida tax system has been geared perhaps unevenly, but on the whole quite well, to the economy of the state. We have done an excellent job of shifting a large portion of the tax burden to tourists—the tax system is designed to tax the services industries quite heavily. The change in the character and make-up of Florida's population and its economic structure will, no doubt, force change in the tax system.

PART THREE

Tax Sharing

THE POLITICS AND ECONOMICS OF INTERGOVERNMENTAL FISCAL RELATIONS:
Federal Grants, Tax Credits, and Revenue Sharing

DEIL S. WRIGHT

A CURRENT POPULAR PASTIME among public officials and academics is the leveling of criticisms against the growth and proliferation of federal categorical grants-in-aid. With more than 400 separate authorizations, 170 major programs, elaborate application and granting procedures, and budgeted levels at $20.3 billion for fiscal 1969, it is little wonder that we have a rash of commentaries with a critical bent. If trends persist, gunning for grants will rival another restricted sport—shooting fish in a barrel. Many criticisms of grants are justly deserved. But this essay intends to contribute less to the hue and cry against the present state of affairs and more to the descriptive exposition of constructive policy alternatives.

The focal points for the paper are two broad issues: (1) improvements in the existing form and structure of federal grants, and (2) a review of two major alternatives to grants—the tax credit and tax sharing. This discussion occurs in the context of two highly significant qualifying conditions, the Viet Nam War and President Lyndon Johnson's "creative federalism." The harsh fiscal and non-fiscal realities of our policies in Southeast Asia cause a continuous rethinking and revision of domestic policy directions. But optimism, if nothing else, suggests that we look toward a time when more viable fiscal policy choices are open than the tension-ridden ones that now confront the nation. The second major constraint on this discussion is the rhetoric and practice of creative federalism. Based on evidence beyond and tangential to the focus of this paper, it seems clear that the realities of creative federalism

An earlier version of this paper was presented at the meetings of the Southern Economic Association, New Orleans, Louisiana, November 16–18, 1967. Portions of the paper are also drawn from a monograph titled Federal Grants-in-Aid: Perspectives and Alternatives (Washington, D.C.: American Enterprise Institute, 1968).

are pinned on two action orientations: (1) an extensive expansion of existing and new categorical grants, and (2) the wholesale extension of project-type funding authorizations that are more narrowly specified than even the categorical program grants.

How can the manageability and coordination of federal grants be improved? A number of approaches have been suggested, and some experimental efforts have been made to institute a few of these proposed changes. For convenience and clarity these improvements may be listed and discussed under three headings: congressional policy, executive branch structure, and administrative procedure. These classifications, it should be added, are not rigid compartmentalizations.

Congressional Policy

Among the several proposals to alter congressional policy and approach to grants, the so-called "consolidated" grant approach has been prominent for many years. This idea evolved largely as a response to the number of Depression-born categorical programs enacted in the health and welfare fields. It has been mentioned frequently and examined occasionally as a means of overcoming the increasingly specialized and fragmented characteristics of categorical grants.[1] The consolidated grant retains the conditional and matching features of standard grants. The strings attached to expenditures are restrictive only in relation to function and not to particular subcategories or programs within a broad functional field. For example, instead of giving federal support to four or five categories of eligible welfare recipients, a single general grant for welfare would be substituted.

The proposal for consolidated grants has languished in academic literature and in the policy suggestion stage for many years. Finally, in 1966, a significant breakthrough occurred with the en-

---

[1] The term consolidated grant has sometimes been called "block" grant. For a brief essay clearly distinguishing between block and consolidated grants see George C. S. Benson and Harold F. McClelland, *Consolidated Grants: A Means of Maintaining Fiscal Responsibility* (American Enterprise Institute, 1961).

actment of P.L. 89–749.[2] This legislation, titled "Comprehensive Health Care Planning and Services Act," eliminated more than a dozen categorical public health formula grants to the states for such specific programs as cancer, heart disease, mental illness, venereal diseases, neurological diseases, and community health services and substituted a single grant for comprehensive health care services. The amount authorized under the single grant was $62.5 million annually in contrast to about $50 million under the several categorical grants.

An added dimension of this particular "experiment" with the consolidated grant approach was the condition that each state create or designate an agency with responsibility for developing comprehensive plans of health services. These plans are expected to provide for careful distribution of state and federal funds among the various health services and to constitute the basis for federal review of state health programing. Two other aspects of this legislation are worth noting. First, there is a declared administrative intent to designate significant decision-making activities to the regional offices and thereby reduce the frequent administrative necessity of "many trips to Washington." As the federal official responsible for the administration of this program stated recently, "The Regional Office will be where the action is." [3] Second, accompanying the new single grant program was a project grant program supportive of areawide health planning. The specific project character of this grant has an important saving grace. The use of project grants, which are awarded on a regional or local basis, is required to be related to the state's comprehensive health care

---

[2] S. 3008, 89th Congress; Public Law 89–749, 89th Congress, November 3, 1966; *Comprehensive Health Planning and Public Health Services Amendments of 1966*, 89th Congress, 2nd Session, Senate Report No. 1665, September 29, 1966; and *Comprehensive Health Planning and Public Health Services Amendments of 1966*, Hearing before the Committee on Interstate and Foreign Commerce, House of Representatives, 89th Congress, 2nd Session, October 11, 1966.

[3] Address by James H. Cavanaugh, director, Office of Comprehensive Health Planning and Development, U.S. Public Health Service, presented at the 4th annual Institute for the Staffs of Areawide Planning Agencies, University of Chicago, Chicago, Illinois, December 12, 1966.

planning program. P.L. 89–749 is an important positive step in the federal grant field. Its enactment commands attention, its intent is highly laudable, and its results will deserve careful study for new points of departure in improving grant programs.

There is, however, a *lack* of consistency among grant programs in two respects, grant allocation formulas and matching requirements. The variations in apportionment formulas and matching requirements have grown like Topsy with no general rationale and little concern for the formulas in other related grants. The Advisory Commission on Intergovernmental Relations (ACIR) studied this general problem as it related specifically to the equalization objectives of grants.[4] It found, for example, that the maximum federal matching percentage varied from 66.67 through 82.9 for thirteen different variable matching grant programs. For sixteen equalization grants that incorporated state fiscal capacity into the apportionment formulas, the proportion of each grant distributed on the basis of fiscal capacity varied from 17.8 per cent to 100 per cent. Of the sixteen grants only four had similar proportions (100 per cent) distributed on the basis of fiscal capacity. These variations led the commission to recommend that practicable equalization provisions, introduced through both allocation and matching requirements, should aim for a reasonable, uniform level of minimum program performance in every state, that uniformity in the mechanics of the equalization provisions was preferable to variety, and that statutory specification was more desirable than administrative discretion. Secondly, the ACIR recommended that departments and agencies charged with the administration of federal grant programs be required by the President to review periodically the adequacy of the need indexes employed in their respective grant programs and the appropriateness of their equalization provisions, and that this review be coordinated by the Bureau of the Budget.[5]

---

[4] *The Role of Equalization in Federal Grants* (Washington, 1964), 39–43.
[5] *Ibid.*, 77, 79.

If consolidation of grants is not feasible, then consistency in allocation and matching formulas among similar grants is an important secondary means of improvement. There are two chief difficulties associated with efforts to mobilize coordinated congressional action on grants. First, grants originate in and are acted on by several different substantive committees in the House and Senate. Congressional specialization via the committee structure, then, inhibits some consistency and coordination in the enactment of grant programs. Second, the Congress has not explicitly imposed on itself the duty of a regularized review of grant programs. Grant programs are enacted for varying lengths of time with few precise indications of objectives that can be examined or evaluated from the standpoint of meeting stated needs. Of course, annual review by means of the budget and appropriations process occurs regularly. But there are different kinds and levels of review. The marginal character of the annual budget examination plus the growing number and diversity of grants has stimulated considerable recent interest in what has been called "periodic review." This review proposal, usually designated to occur at five-year intervals, has been popularized by both the House and Senate Intergovernmental Relations Subcommittees and by the Advisory Commission on Intergovernmental Relations.[6]

The commission, for example, strongly urges the appropriate congressional committees to ask basic rather than marginal questions concerning the purposes and the accomplishments of grants. This type of fundamental review has its analog in the budgetary

---

[6] *Federal-State-Local Relations: Federal Grants-In-Aid*, Thirtieth Report by the Committee on Government Operations, 85th Congress, 2nd Session, House Report 2533, August 8, 1958; *Congressional Review of Federal Grants-In-Aid*, Hearings before a Subcommittee of the Committee on Government Operations, House of Representatives, 87th Congress, 1st Session, July 25 and 27, 1961; *Periodic Congressional Review of Federal Grants-In-Aid*, Hearings before the Subcommittee on Intergovernmental Relations of the Committee on Government Operations, U.S. Senate, 88th Congress, 2nd Session, January 14, 15, and 16, 1964; Advisory Commission on Intergovernmental Relations, *Periodic Congressional Reassessment of Federal Grants-In-Aid to State and Local Governments*, June, 1961.

sphere where it would be comprehensive or zero-based in contrast to the existing incremental approach.[7] Under the annual budget review procedures now used, grant programs are subject only to incremental analysis. Furthermore, and most significantly, it would appear that the extension and expansion of grant programs is presently subject to incremental rather than even moderately comprehensive analysis. The ACIR noted that in instances where basic review had been undertaken "efforts to redirect grant programs toward newer and more urgent problems within a given program area usually result in an *additive* rather than a *substitutive* appropriation." [8] Review and redirection in the grant field has meant in practice, therefore, the automatic and cumulative continuation without regard to purpose or need of nearly all grants once they achieve statutory status. The proposal for five-year periodic review of grants is similar to the idea advanced by Wildavsky in his "radical incremental" approach to the budget process.[9]

Executive Branch Structure

If grant review, management, and coordination are to be improved, then some actions are required within the executive branch itself. The thrust of these changes should help to offset some of the negative tendencies identified in the attitudes of federal aid officials, namely, functionalism, professionalism, protectionism, and indifference.[10] In short, there should be located at critical points in federal administration, key individuals who, by reason of background and outlook, will ask questions and act intelligently from an intergovernmental standpoint. A ten-point program outlined by Senator Edmund Muskie of Maine suggests

[7] For a discussion of budgetary incrementalism, see Aaron Wildavsky, *The Politics of the Budgetary Process* (Boston: Little Brown, 1964).

[8] *Periodic Congressional Reassessment*, 22.

[9] See Aaron Wildavsky, "Toward a Radical Incrementalism: A Proposal to Aid Congress in Reform of the Budgetary Process," in *Congress: The First Branch of Government* (Washington, D.C.: American Enterprise Institute, 1966), 115–65.

[10] *The Federal System as Seen by Federal Aid Officials*, Subcommittee on Intergovernmental Relations of the Committee on Government Operations, U.S. Senate, 89th Congress, 1st Session (Committee Print), December 15, 1965.

why the executive branch has failed to choose a staff that could build into the federal administrative system a genuine concern for intergovernmental relationships.[11] The pressure toward "functional government" at the federal level has far overshadowed a deliberate weighing of the consequences of functionalism on state and local governments.[12] Functionalism has also been the basis of what former Senator Kenneth Keating of New York used to describe as "Federal fiscal reflex." By this term he characterized the disposition of the executive branch, supported by Congress, to discover a problem and then throw money at it, hoping that it would somehow go away.

The several proposals for partially reorienting the executive branch deserve further study and more detailed evaluation. It is rare that executive reorganization proposals originate in the legislative branch and rarer still that they are implemented through legislative leadership. At a minimum we can hope that Senator Muskie's suggestions will cause the executive branch to give serious and broad-gauged consideration to how it might better retool itself for the domestic challenges ahead. Again the senator perceptively put his finger on a critical aspect of the great society and creative federalism dilemma: "During the past two Congresses we have concentrated primarily on the substance of government; now the spotlight must be turned on [structure and] procedure."

Administrative Procedure

In addition to legislative policy and executive structure, administrative procedures offer promising prospects for the improvement of federal grants. Six specific changes oriented toward procedural improvement (but having obvious policy implications) were recommended by the ACIR, drafted in legislative form, reviewed in hearings, and passed by the Senate in 1966. The Senate legislation

[11] See *Congressional Record* (Daily Edition), March 25, 1966.
[12] For a brief discussion of "functional government" including the threats it poses and the necessities for civic action, see Committee for Economic Development, *Modernizing Local Government*, a statement by the Research and Policy Committee, July, 1966.

(S. 561) was titled "Intergovernmental Cooperation Act of 1965," [13] and embodied not only procedural changes but also provisions for periodic review of grants, for coordination of metropolitan and urban development, for areawide review and comment on applications for grants in metropolitan areas (a title that was subsequently inserted into the Demonstration Cities Act), and for policies governing the use and disposition of federally owned land in urban areas. We will focus only on the more procedurally oriented aspects of this legislation.

One provision is intended to foster the full disclosure to governors or other state officials of information on the federal funds received by state departments and agencies. This information would be furnished at the governor's request, and the legislation explicitly indicates (Sec. 101) that "no act of Congress shall be construed to prevent the governor or other designated officer from participating in the state's determination of its financial needs in the same manner as he does with respect to the budgeting of state funds." This approach to administrative improvement of grants at the state level is based on Bacon's aphorism, "knowledge is power." Greater information in the hands of political and administrative generalists should help to reduce the insulation and autonomy of program administrators. As of 1965 a survey of forty-one state budget directors revealed that in only fourteen states were all the requests for and receipt of federal funds channeled through customary state fiscal review procedures.[14] In Massachusetts the extremities of independence were attained by state public and mental health personnel. Four *private* corporations were established to obtain federal (and other) funds completely free from state controls despite the fact that the corporation president was

[13] *Intergovernmental Cooperation Act of 1965*, Hearings before the Subcommittee on Intergovernmental Relations of the Committee on Government Operations, U.S. Senate, 89th Congress, 1st Session, March 29, 30, 31, and April 1, 2, 1965; *Intergovernmental Cooperation Act of 1965*, Senate Report No. 538, 89th Congress, 1st Session, August 3, 1965; and *Intergovernmental Cooperation*, Hearings before a Subcommittee of the Committee on Government Operations, House of Representatives, 89th Congress, 2nd Session, March 1, 2, 8, 9 and October 5 and 18, 1966.

[14] *Intergovernmental Cooperation Act of 1965*, Hearings, 347.

the state health commissioner and five of the six members of the corporation's administrative committee were employed by the state department of health.

A second procedural improvement is intended to reinforce the former one. It provides that all federal grant funds shall be paid to the state treasurer or other designated state official rather than directly to a particular agency or other special accounts. Permissive language allows the states to permit direct receipt of federal funds by state institutions of higher learning. A closely related third improvement is the requirement that no federal funds may be deposited in separate bank accounts but shall be deposited with the other monies administered by the state. The significance of this arrangement is that the state's fiscal officer will draw on and obtain federal funds as needed rather than numerous separate agencies receiving the funds. An associated fourth improvement concerns the orderly and timely scheduling of the transfers of funds to be used by the states. Improved scheduling would eliminate the long-standing debate about the interest earned on grant funds transferred to state governments prior to the need to finance expenditure.

The main intent of these proposals is not to force states to conform to a particular accounting or budgeting scheme but to make it much easier, if a state desires, to enact supplementary legislation that would help centralize fiscal control and information of federal funds at the state level. Enactment of these improvements would remove some impediments and friction from federal-state fiscal operations.

Grant Alternatives

Even if an ironclad case could be made against grants, from a practical standpoint they are an institutionalized part of the federal system with a half-century of solid precedent. Their level and proliferation in recent years have imposed strains and engendered conflicts within the federal system. In the prior section we identified some possible courses of action for combatting these consequences. Here we will consider possible financial mechanisms that could be used instead of compounding the existing strains and conflicts by adding more categorical grant programs. The necessity for discussing these alternatives has been aptly summarized by the observation: national progress bestows both bounties and burdens: the bounties tend to be national, the burdens state and local. In short, prosperity provides the federal treasury with revenues, but the problems and demands tend to concentrate at the state-local levels. The question we address here is: How, other than by the much-used grant device, might the gap be bridged between revenue raising and spending demands? Four alternatives will be discussed, and major attention will be accorded the Heller plan for revenue sharing with the states.

Direct Federal Expenditures. One way of alleviating the fiscal pressures at the state-local level would be the direct assumption of responsibility by the national government for a variety of public programs. The problem of medical assistance for the aged, for example, was ultimately resolved in this fashion although the grant technique was originally and rather unsuccessfully employed. This approach, while most appealing to political liberals, does not square well with most of our experience in providing the bulk of civilian functions of government through state and local units. If the snail's pace speed with which medicare was passed by Congress is any indication of the disposition for direct federal action, states and local units might be inundated with problems and/or tied in fiscal knots by the time federal "relief" is forthcoming. From a political standpoint, then, it seems unlikely that wholesale federal assumption of problem responsibilities is likely to occur.

Federal Tax Reduction. Tax reduction holds a broad-based appeal for many public officials as well as the tax conscious citizenry. It also occupies a special status among conservatives because of all the federal fiscal policy measures it gives the greatest amount of responsibility to individuals and firms in the private sector. In what way is it an alternative to more grants-in-aid? How do federal tax cuts add to the amount of revenues obtained by states and local units? A cut produces state-local revenues in both direct and indirect ways. Most of this tends to come indirectly from the economic expansion generated by the tax reduction. But some increased state revenues come directly from additions to the tax base in those nineteen states that allow federal income taxes paid as a deductible item on the state income tax. What is the state-local sector revenue gain from federal tax reduction? Professor Walter Heller indicates that "an estimated $3 billion extra a year is flowing into state-local coffers from the 1964 tax cut alone, a 7 per cent increase for both state and local tax revenues." [15] If his estimate is correct then the federal tax cut was responsible for nearly 90 per cent of the $3.5 billion in added tax revenue obtained by the state-local sector in fiscal 1965 over 1964![16] This is an unusually high proportion, but most state legislatures were not in session in 1964 to enact tax increases effective in fiscal 1965. The percentage is not as unreasonable as it might seem.

There is an additional way in which federal tax reduction may indirectly benefit the fiscal position of the state-local sector. Lower federal taxes do provide an opportunity for the nonfederal sector to take up the slack by increasing state or local taxes. The action-reaction was once characterized by columnist James Reston as "the President giveth and the governors taketh away." Unfortunately, we have no known systematic studies on which to base the estimated impact of this phenomenon. If the broad excise tax cuts of 1965 are a gauge of the inclination "for the states to rush in where the Federal angel no longer treads," then no significant fiscal relief is in sight for the state-local sector.[17]

While federal tax reduction offers a solution to the ills of state and local treasuries, it has several important limitations. The primary one, of course, is that federal tax reductions are dictated by economic and political considerations that are far removed from

[15] Walter W. Heller, *New Dimensions of Political Economy* (Cambridge, Mass.: Harvard University Press, 1966), 140.
[16] U.S. Bureau of the Census, *Governmental Finances* in 1964–65, Series GF-No. 6 (Revised, February, 1967), 18.
[17] Heller, *New Dimensions of Political Economy*, 140.

state-local revenue factors. Simply put, increased state and local revenues are a *consequence* of tax cuts rather than a primary or even secondary justification for reduction. Seen in this light, and despite its attractiveness, federal tax reduction cannot be considered a major mechanism for adjusting the fiscal problems of federalism nor as a likely alternative to increased federal grants.

Tax Credits. A tax credit, in contrast to tax deductibility, is a reduction in tax liability to the full extent of the allowable credit. Two venerable and well-known examples of the tax credit in federal-state relations are the death tax credit and the unemployment insurance tax credit. Their use has been thoroughly institutionalized, debated, and evaluated.[18] Seven states have experimented with the tax credit primarily to offer tax relief to economically disadvantaged groups. Colorado, Hawaii, and Indiana allowed per person tax credits (positive and negative) against the taxpayer's state income tax liability to afford relief from the regressivity of sales taxes, especially on food. Wisconsin adopted this device as a means of giving property tax relief to senior citizens. These new ventures at the state level have much to commend them, especially on economic and administrative grounds. There has been more and more serious thought given to their applicability to the federal-state scene. For example, the ACIR recommended that the Internal Revenue Code be amended "on a prospective basis to give income taxpayers an option to either (a) continue itemizing their income tax payments to State and local governments or (b) claim a substantial percentage of such payments as a credit against their Federal income tax liability." [19] The purpose of the (a) proviso is to permit taxpayers in the high marginal tax rate brackets to continue deductibility in those instances where a greater tax saving occurs than under a "substantial" credit.

---

[18] James A. Maxwell, *Tax Credits and Intergovernmental Fiscal Relations* (Washington, D.C.: The Brookings Institution, 1962).

[19] Advisory Commission on Intergovernmental Relations, *Federal-State Coordination of Personal Income Taxes*, October, 1965, p. 19.

There appear to be three major advantages of the commission's tax credit proposal. First is its combined ease, simplicity, and high degree of taxpayer visibility. In bold and stark black-and-white print on Form 1040, the taxpayer would be informed that he should specify all state-local income taxes paid, take 40 per cent of that amount (for example), and then *subtract* that product from his previously calculated federal tax bill.

A second asset is the incentive or effort-oriented bias of the proposal. In contrast to the traditional tax credit as a ceiling percentage of the *federal* tax liability, this idea ties the credited percentage to the state-local income tax liability. Thus, no matter how high state and local income taxes rise, 40 per cent of that amount could be subtracted from the federal tax. This approach does not inhibit but positively stimulates state-local effort in the income tax field.

The third chief asset of this plan is its income base. Since the income tax is among the most responsive of all taxes to economic growth there is a supplementary revenue growth factor built into this proposal. States could more assuredly hitch their tax revenue wagons to the rising star of national economic growth.

Against these advantages must be weighted at least three important limitations: first, the plan faces difficult political realities —fifteen states do not currently have income taxes; second, the device allows for no interstate equalization of fiscal burdens; and last, it would provide an initial windfall benefit to the taxpayers, rather than to state-local governments in those jurisdictions already taxing income (thirty-five states).

Tax Sharing. The shared revenue device has played an incidental and nearly insignificant role in federal-state fiscal relations. Nine shared revenue programs exist exclusively in the natural resources field, and these amounted to less than $200 million in 1968. American avoidance of tax sharing and near-exclusive reliance on the conditional grant is in sharp contrast to the intergovernmental fiscal mechanisms employed by other federal systems. For example, in Australia about three fourths of all federal fiscal aids to the states are in the form of unrestricted general revenue payments based on income tax collections.[20] Likewise, Canada relies heavily on a type of revenue sharing with its provincial governments, moving only in recent years toward more conditional grants of the type we have termed grants-in-aid.[21] The reasons for such contrasts need not detain us. Instead, we propose to describe briefly some of the recently discussed proposals for federal tax sharing with the states and to examine the pros and cons of tax sharing. We will conclude with a few summary observations on how it fits the criteria for making federalism more effective in the United States.

The Heller-Pechman Plan

The idea of tax or revenue sharing has been most closely associated with Professor Walter Heller, economist and chairman of the Council of Economic Advisors from 1961–64. In his most recent and complete exposition of the plan Heller calls it "per capita revenue sharing." [22] The purpose is to set aside a substantial amount of money from federal revenues to be returned to the states with minimal restrictions on the allocation of the funds. The immediate aim is to relieve state-local fiscal pressures, but ancillary intents often involve fiscal equalization, improvement of income distributions, and generally strengthening the autonomy and viability of the nonfederal sector. There are five pertinent operational aspects: form, base, amount, distribution formula, and conditions.

There seems to be considerable agreement that funds from revenue sharing, whatever the base and amount derived, should be formally placed in a trust fund from which the distributions to the states would be made. The trust fund arrangement would have several advantages. It would represent a type of contractual understanding by the federal government that the funds are due

[20] Albert J. Robinson, "Implementing Policies of Growth and Stability in a Federation," *National Tax Journal*, XVIII (March, 1965), 63.

[21] R. M. Burns, "Intergovernmental Relations in Canada: Further Developments," *National Tax Journal*, XVIII (March, 1965), 15–24.

[22] Heller, *New Dimensions of Political Economy*, 144–72.

the states as a matter of right rather than as discretionary largess subject to the vagaries of the annual appropriation process. This would also clearly separate revenue sharing from traditional grants-in-aid, to the benefit of both types of aid. It would constitute a prior claim, a fractional tithe, upon federal funds in advance of tax reduction, debt retirement, etc. In this respect the revenue sharing is less conservative in outlook. On the other hand, it is more conservative than direct federal expenditures or grants-in-aid.

Varying suggestions have been made for the base on which revenue sharing would be calculated. Three alternatives have been proposed: (1) all federal revenues, (2) federal personal income tax collections, and (3) the federal personal income tax base. The income tax base would be larger, more constantly growing, and less subject to sharp variations than the other two alternatives.

How much could be raised and returned to the states? The amount obviously would be the product of a specified rate applied to a given base. Thus, in 1966 a 1 per cent rate applied to the federal individual income tax base would have yielded $2.8 billion for a revenue sharing trust fund. The Republican Coordinating Committee estimated that a 2 per cent rate (applied to all income tax collections) effective during fiscal 1967 would have provided about $2 billion.[23]

An increasing rate during the first few years of revenue sharing has considerable appeal and more than a modicum of merit. It would provide a valuable build-up capacity that the states could rely on over and above revenues from economic growth. It would also make sense to start with a low rate and increase it gradually to permit orderly rather than sudden fiscal management and allocation choices at the state level. The Heller plan contemplates such an escalating rate during the first years of the plan. A rate designed to produce approximately $2 billion in the beginning and escalating to one that would provide about $6 billion in six to

[23] Republican Coordinating Committee, *Financing the Future of Federalism: The Case For Revenue Sharing* (Washington, D.C.: Republican National Committee, March, 1966).

eight years (about $30 per capita available for distribution) would seem satisfactory.

A wide range of criteria has been suggested to guide officials in parceling out the revenue among states. A few of the more prominent ones are division (1) on the basis of federal income taxes paid by taxpayers within the state, (2) on the basis of population (per capita), and (3) on the basis of various combinations of population, personal income, and tax effort. Clearly, the pattern of distribution makes a great difference in the amounts (or proportions) that specific states receive. With the first alternative, federal income taxes, there would be no equalization whatsoever. Geographic redistribution would not occur. In fact, very few of the proposals seriously discussed for revenue sharing urge the primary use of this criterion.[24] Professor Heller prefers a basis of population as the guide to distribution—"per capita revenue sharing." Variations from a per capita formula have been proposed by Senator Jacob Javits and by Congressman Charles Goodell. They would set aside, respectively, 20 per cent and 10 per cent of the trust fund to be separately allocated to either one-fourth or one-third of the states with lowest per capita personal incomes. These proposals provide a greater degree of equalization than that resulting from the simple per capita formula by giving an added "bonus" to the low-income states.

The extent of equalization resulting from the use of different allocator components in distribution formulas may be seen in Table 3. It is apparent that revenue sharing on the basis of federal personal income taxes produces reverse equalization. The ten states with highest per capita incomes would get back in the form of unrestricted revenues .2375 per cent of the total personal income in those states. However, the ten states with lowest per capita incomes would receive as unrestricted revenues only .1714 per cent of their total personal income under this criterion.

[24] The Republican Coordinating Committee recommended that one half of the shared revenues be distributed on the basis of income taxes and the other half on a combination of population and personal income.

Distribution according to population sharply shifts the balance in favor of equalization with the ten highest income states standing at .1756 per cent and the ten lowest at .3124. The greatest equalization is achieved by using a combination of population, personal income, and tax effort. Since the lower income states are also exerting, on the average, greater tax effort, the greater equalizing effect of this criterion can be observed in the final column.

TABLE 3

PERCENTAGE OF 1963 STATE PERSONAL INCOME
OBTAINED BY STATES (IN QUINTILE INCOME GROUPS)
FROM A HYPOTHETICAL $1 BILLION REVENUE
SHARING PROGRAM BASED ON FOUR
DISTRIBUTIONAL CRITERIA

States Ranked by Per Capita Personal Income	Distributional Criterion			
	Federal Income Tax	Population	Population and Personal Income	Population Personal Income and Tax Effort
	(average percentage of personal income from revenue sharing)			
1st Quintile	.2375	.1756	.1355	.1270
2nd Quintile	.2143	.2152	.2039	.2053
3rd Quintile	.1949	.2366	.2445	.2738
4th Quintile	.1801	.2656	.3114	.3518
5th Quintile	.1714	.3124	.4376	.4552

Source: Adapted from George F. Break, *Intergovernmental Fiscal Relations in the United States* (Brookings, 1966), 259.

A final and complex aspect of the revenue sharing plan deals with conditions to be or not to be attached to the use of the funds by the states. Here the nature and impetus of the plan dictate that the strings attached to spending the money be held to an absolute minimum. But what is the "absolute minimum"? Generally, little disagreement exists over the necessity and desirability of requiring reports from the states (*not* detailed audits) on how the money is spent. The consensus is that Title VI of the Civil Rights Act of 1964 should prevent the funds from being used to foster or maintain segregation. Another popularly sought limitation is one to keep these funds from being used for highway purposes since a federal trust fund and user revenues are already dedicated to that function. Beyond this point, however, a wide variety of particular preferences and special perspectives take shape.

Pros & Cons of the Plan

Revenue sharing has been discussed with such frequency and vigor recently that the advantages and disadvantages of the plan have taken definite shape.

ARGUMENTS FOR REVENUE SHARING

1. *Simplicity.* The plan is straightforward, clear, and direct in its conception and operation.

2. *State discretion.* It provides the states with more discretion and greater fiscal autonomy to meet the particular needs as those needs are judged by state (and local) officials.

3. *Major needs.* Revenue sharing is not a stop-gap measure but puts substantial funds in the coffers of those governments that face the major responsibilities for civilian services.

4. *Equalization.* In its simplest per capita distribution form it would equalize income and tax effort variations among the states and in this respect would function far more effectively than grants-in-aid. It can also be adjusted easily to produce greater equalization than straight per capita distribution provides.

5. *Revenue growth.* Not only would revenue sharing furnish major sums but the revenue returns, hitched closely to economic growth, would automatically increase at a pace greater than the growth rate.

6. *Flexibility.* The simplicity of the plan fosters flexibility. The base, rate, amount, and distribution criteria can be employed to achieve precise and explicit policy goals.

7. *Revitalization.* Adoption of the plan would give the states and local units a healthy fiscal shot-in-the-arm. It would enhance public confidence in state and local government by better enabling them to meet public demands.

8. *Progressivity-regressivity.* The plan would have the effect of financing a greater share of state and local services out of progressively levied federal income taxes (or tax base) rather than from regressive sales, consumer, and property taxes.

9. *Grant relief.* Enactment of revenue sharing is likely to forestall further major grant-in-aid programs and in so doing, prevent more proliferation, complexity, and problems in the grant field. Whether revenue sharing would eventually replace or supplant existing grants is an open question.

10. *Economic stabilization.* Revenue sharing would tie a portion of state-local receipts and outlays to the business cycle and provide an additional built-in compensator, especially in time of recession when the countercyclical effects of state-local finance are stabilizing.

11. *Reduced skewing.* By providing relatively unrestricted funds to the states, revenue sharing would constitute a major step in reducing (or compensating for) the skewing effect on state budgets brought about by federal grants-in-aid.

12. *Fiscal drag.* Tax sharing would have the effect of reducing the "fiscal drag" on the economy (prior to Viet Nam) brought on by surplus federal revenues. Should the costs of our world commitments be reduced a powerful case could be made for revenue sharing.

13. *Red tape reduction.* The ease and simplicity of revenue sharing hold to a minimum the administrative overhead costs involved where grants or other federal aids are involved. One study of the administrative costs of grants placed the overhead percentage on ten grant programs at about 1.6 per cent. If this percentage applied across the board then about $300 million in federal funds are consumed in collecting and administering grant-in-aid funds. This conservative estimate does not count the compliance costs at the state level for administering grants. It is clear that revenue sharing would keep federal-state overhead costs to a bare minimum.

14. *Pro-poor.* One result of placing federally raised funds in state-local expenditure hands is that the net effect will be more in favor of the economically disadvantaged in our society. State and local expenditures are known to be heavily beneficial to lower income groups. Furthermore, the net budget (*i.e.*, tax incidence and expenditure benefits) of the state-local sector is estimated to be more pro-poor than is the federal tax-expenditure budget. Revenue sharing would solidify this pattern.

15. *Attitudinally acceptable.* Not only is revenue sharing accept-

able to the public at large but also it fits well with the varied and mixed perspectives of officials connected with existing grant programs. It has the further saving grace of not directly threatening any solidified power bloc. What it needs is a solid pro-state lobby behind it. Only the governors can furnish such support, and there is some indication that they are moving more in the direction of unified active support for revenue sharing. Except for the governors, however, one can ask the question: Who lobbies for the states in Washington? The answer seems to be: Nobody!

16. *Ample precedent.* The existence of tax sharing in other countries, at the state-local level in this country, and in infinitesimal form at the federal-state level provides examples and experience upon which to draw in undertaking full-fledged consideration of revenue sharing. The House Ways and Means Committee and the Senate Finance Committee should schedule full-scale hearings on the plan at the earliest possible date and obtain testimony from federal, state, and local officials plus knowledgeable academic personages and private and quasi-public interest groups.

ARGUMENTS AGAINST REVENUE SHARING

1. *National drain.* Giving funds to the states would take needed funds away from federal purposes where they could be put to better use than at the state-local level. In its most extreme form the argument is, "If the federal government spends it, it must be good!"

2. *Leaky purses.* This is the other side of the national drain coin. Revenue sharing with the states would put money in leaky purses. States do not exercise care, responsibility, and foresight in their outlays. The most trenchant expression of this view appeared in an article titled "Why Bail Out the States?" where Christopher Jencks came out against the Heller plan because the states were "unfit to govern" and represented "a kind of cancer."

3. *Reduced effort.* More money to the states under revenue sharing will cause them to reduce their tax efforts at a time when they most need to strengthen their fiscal fortitude.

4. *Local needs.* Tax sharing, by giving money directly to the states, fails completely to recognize the pressing fiscal needs of our large cities and urban areas that traditionally have gotten short shift from state legislatures. Reapportionment, it is argued,

will not help much because suburbia, not central cities, has gained better representation.

5. *Rathole theory.* Even if substantial amounts of money trickle down to the local level from revenue sharing much of it will go down the rathole of local government overlapping, duplication, mismanagement, and just plain waste. We are currently applying the rathole theory of local finance whereby we pump more and more money down a hole that contains a suspected problem, hoping someday that the hole will be plugged.

6. *Waste and inefficiency.* An inclination similar to the rathole theory functions at the state level except that the states are not as well organized and professionalized as at the local (city) level. Without the skills to find the ratholes at the state level revenue sharing would simply compound confusion, waste, and ineffectiveness.

7. *Tax reform.* By putting more money in the states' hands through revenue sharing, the pressure to bring about much-needed state (and local) tax reforms would be greatly reduced. The only way to get these reforms is to keep the pressure on, even if it means precipitating fiscal crises and occasional near-bankruptcies.

8. *Grant cuts.* Increased state revenues via tax sharing might generate skepticism regarding old as well as new grants. The spread of such skepticism might undermine existing grant programs.

9. *Responsibility.* Under tax sharing the responsibility for revenue raising will be divorced from spending authority. Such a split is inherently bad because it fails to keep the spending unit "honest" in terms of wise expenditures and responsibility to the people (on whom it depends less for raising money). The responsibility for overseeing expenditures is one of the factors that has caused Congress to look with favor on grants-in-aid: it can specify in detail and with reasonable precision what happens to the money.

10. *Tax reduction.* This argument says that revenue sharing is not needed, it is just another way to pluck the goose with the least amount of squawking. All taxes are too high. What is needed is tax reduction before revenue sharing.

11. *Debt reduction.* This viewpoint is essentially the same as

the former one except that debt reduction is given the priority previously occupied by tax reduction and revenue sharing falls outside the scope of significant priorities.

12. *Prosperity presumed.* Tax sharing rests heavily on the presumption of continuous prosperity tied in with a federal surplus. Prosperity is by no means assured, this argument asserts. Furthermore, we have had only one balanced budget (either administrative or cash consolidated) in the past decade so it is spurious to talk about sharing a non-existent "surplus" with the states.

Revenue sharing comes off the better of all possible alternatives to grants-in-aid. The unique tax credit device from the ACIR is the second preferred alternative. Revenue sharing is simple. It is consistent with a body of attitudinal perspectives distributed among officials and the public in our federal system. It recognizes the interrelatedness of federal-state-local financial systems. It seeks to deal with our interconnected fiscal system in a manner calculated to preserve and broaden the autonomy of the states. It holds out the excellent prospect of a better federal system by enhancing the existing strengths of the states. The question, as Walter Heller has put it, is this simple: "Do you want stronger states?" One vote here is cast in the affirmative.

Concluding Observations

The theoretical base for fiscal equity within a federal system has been adequately argued by James Buchanan.[25] He demonstrates that the policy objective of equality formulated in interpersonal terms can be served through interstate fiscal equalization. Buchanan also notes the inconsistency present in the fact that the states are integrated parts of a national economy but as governmental units they are forced to act as if their respective economies were fiscally separate and independent. In this connection a reference is made to the "revenue sharing" proposal made by

[25] James M. Buchanan, "Federalism and Fiscal Equity," in *Fiscal Theory and Political Economy* (Chapel Hill: University of North Carolina Press, 1960), 170–89.

William H. Jones in 1887.[26] Jones proposed a system of centrally collected taxes shared on a per capita basis among the states. In short, revenue sharing is not a novel idea, and there is strong justification in equity terms for unconditional equalizing grants to the states. The inclusion of state-local tax effort as an apportionment factor in the distribution formula would contribute further to equity aims. It would also reduce the likelihood that states would use the unrestricted funds for tax reduction or foregone tax increases, countering the charge that the states should not be rewarded for failing to use their own fiscal capacities to the fullest extent. With or without a tax effort component built into the distribution, unconditional grants would be a major step in achieving equalization objectives that are not now even approximated by categorical and conditional grants.

The contrasting impact between current grants and proposed unconditional grants was recently identified by James Plummer.[27] He found a positive correlation of .09 in 1964 between per capita personal income and per capita federal grants to the states. Revenue sharing on the basis of a population-tax effort formula was correlated with per capita personal income at—.274. If 10 per cent of the funds were distributed among the seventeen poorest states and the remainder allocated on the population-effort basis the correlation rises to—.708.[28] Only slight adjustments are necessary, then, to produce powerful equalizing effects in unconditional grants.

Perhaps the greatest deterrent to the adoption of revenue sharing stems from distrust and doubt concerning the responsibility of the states. Elsewhere, I have examined the strengths and weaknesses of the states and observed that the former outweigh the latter from the standpoints of political tendencies and traditions,

[26] *Ibid.*, 178.

[27] James L. Plummer, "Federal-State Revenue Sharing," *Southern Economic Journal*, XXXIII (July, 1966), 120–26.

[28] *Ibid.*, 125; see also Charles J. Goetz, "Federal Block Grants and the Reactivity Problem," and James L. Plummer, "Federal-State Revenue Sharing: Further Comment," *Southern Economic Journal*, XXXIV (July, 1967), 160–65 and 166–68.

fiscal efforts, administrative capabilities, and institutional position.[29] A remaining limiting condition on the states concerns their structural disabilities.

But major initiative for improved approaches and adjustments to the fiscal and non-fiscal problems of federalism does not rest with the states. If there is any one lesson to be learned from the political pangs of the (Kestnbaum) Commission on Intergovernmental Relations and the scholarly analyses of the late Morton Grodzins, it is that national political institutions, the President, and the Congress, are the basic arbiters of the federal system.[30] Furthermore, the forces of functionalism have fractionated these institutions. The organization of the Congress fails to structure into the legislative decision process ideas and influences centrally relevant to federalism and intergovernmental relations. For example, the House and Senate committees on "Intergovernmental Relations," units that have contributed significantly to understanding and concern for federalism, are subsidiary agents of their respective parent Committees on Government Operations. In addition, these parent committees pack comparatively little political muscle once one recognizes their post hoc role. These committees consider problems and legislation *after* substantive programs have been in operation for varying lengths of time. The fate of revenue sharing, to pursue the example further, will rest with the House Ways and Means Committee and the Senate Finance Committee. Few of us need to be reminded, particularly at this juncture, that Wilbur Mills has several concerns that far out-rank the thought of dispensing more funds from the federal treasury.

When we look past the Congress to the executive branch, we

[29] Deil S. Wright, *Intergovernmental Action on Environmental Policy: The Role of the States* (Institute of Public Administration, Indiana University, Bloomington, Indiana, 1967), and Deil S. Wright, *Federal Grants-In-Aid: Perspectives and Alternatives* (American Enterprise Institute for Policy Research, 1968).

[30] The Commission on Intergovernmental Relations, *Report to the President for Transmittal to the Congress*, June, 1955, esp. pp. 30–33; Morton Grodzins, *The American System: A New View of Government in the United States*, Daniel J. Elazar, ed. (Chicago: Rand McNally, 1966).

find few structural patterns that characterize concern for the complexities of intergovernmental relations. The White House staff, the Bureau of the Budget, and most major agencies are not structured or equipped to deal effectively with the broad aspects of multi-system governance. Senator Muskie's numerous proposals for restructuring national governmental machinery deserve serious consideration. Coordination among federal programs is contingent on the infusion of intergovernmental and other perspectives that alter the unrestrained functionalism prevalent in agency programs.

The single sharp and slightly shrill voice that has made the case for intergovernmental relations respected, articulated, and reasonably well known is that of the Advisory Commission on Intergovernmental Relations. But this agency has legal limits and political disabilities. Its accomplishments, and there are several, arise from its solid research, reasoned inferences, and mature recommendations. But the Advisory Commission does not possess nor can it aggregate the necessary party, policy, and interest group support to achieve much more than marginal adjustments in intergovernmental conflicts. On these "squeak points," as Grodzins so aptly termed them, the commission has performed excellently and admirably.

But revenue sharing, of the type and scope considered in this paper, is a major rather than a marginal change in intergovernmental fiscal relations. The commission's tax credit approach was an effort to grapple with significant fiscal readjustment in the federal system. In spite of its merits and respected endorsements[31] the tax credit approach lacks political appeal on three counts, three counts on which a viable revenue sharing plan might be enacted. These three political touchstones that I see favoring the eventual passage of some form of major revenue sharing are simplicity, attractiveness to state and local elected officials, and party sponsorship.

[31] Committee for Economic Development, *A Fiscal Program for a Balanced Federalism,* statement by the Research and Policy Committee, June, 1967.

THE PROPERTY TAX CASE FOR
FEDERAL TAX SHARING

Dick Netzer

THE INHERENT DEFECTS of the American property tax are serious ones, and under current and prospective conditions there is little hope of correcting them within the traditional framework of state and local government finances. Only a major program of sharing federal revenues with the states affords a reasonable solution—one in which the role of the property tax in American society can be de-emphasized.[1]

The Property Tax in an Urban Society

The American property tax can be appraised sensibly only by examining it in its current context, rather than that of the nineteenth century in which it flowered, and several factors are of critical importance here. First, since ours is an increasingly urbanized society, the tax rests with proportionately more weight on the distinctly urban forms of taxable property, notably nonfarm residences, office buildings, and other urban commercial structures. Second, urbanization is associated with rapid increases in the demand for local public services. State-local tax devices are therefore called upon to divert resources from the private to the public sector, which means rising, not stable, tax rates. Third, the urbanization is occurring in a metropolitan form, not in the form of rapid growth of wholly independent small towns into equally independent cities. The pattern of local government which evolved when urban settlements were scattered and independent thus has produced, in most of the country, complex and fragmented systems of local government within individual metropolitan areas. This leads to major disparities in fiscal needs, fiscal resources, and tax rates. Fourth, within metropolitan areas, the

[1] The property tax is evaluated in my book, *Economics of the Property Tax* (Washington, D.C.: The Brookings Institution, 1966).

most serious problems—those connected with poverty, race, and obsolescence—tend to be concentrated within central cities, many of which are suffering from serious relative declines in their taxable resources. Viewed in this context, the property tax has a number of serious failings.

Poor Administration. The conventional belief is that although the property tax is inherently a sound tax, properly utilized as the major revenue source for nonfederal government units, it is badly administered. My view is that the quality of administration of the property tax is *universally* worse than the quality of administration we have come to expect in connection with income and sales taxes. (The measure of quality here is the extent to which similarly situated taxpayers—as defined by the tax laws—actually do pay identical taxes.) In some jurisdictions, the quality of property tax administration is only moderately worse than the quality of good non-property tax administration; in others, it is abysmally worse. But nowhere does it really match non-property tax administration.

Income Redistribution. On a national basis and within an income range covering 80–90 per cent of the country's households—that is, excluding the very rich and the very poor—the property tax appears to be roughly proportional to income in incidence. However, within individual jurisdictions, especially large heterogeneous ones like the big cities, the incidence of the tax is decidedly regressive, especially its housing component. For example, it is estimated that the residential real estate tax in New York City in 1960–61 absorbed about twice as high a percentage of the incomes of households with below-median incomes as it did of the income of households with above-median incomes.[2] This regressivity *within* jurisdictions makes the property tax a conspicuously poor choice for financing local public services—like public assistance—which are explicitly designed to be redistributive in nature.

[2] See Graduate School of Public Administration, New York University, *Financing Government in New York City* (Final Research Report to the Temporary Commission on City Finances, 1966), 51–53, 161–66.

The property tax is also, in most cases, regressive *among* jurisdictions in a single metropolitan area. That is, effective tax rates tend to be substantially higher in the poorer communities than in the richer ones. This, perhaps, matters little in connection with the financing of purely local services, but makes the property tax an inappropriate support for services in which there is a metropolitan-areawide community of interest, with major interjurisdictional spillovers of benefits and costs.

The Supply of Public Services. These interjurisdictional spillovers provide the basis for what has been called "the undernourishment hypothesis." The argument is that reliance on local tax finance to support public services within a fragmented pattern of government leads to under-financing of public services in metropolitan areas. In part, this is because taxpayers in a single jurisdiction cannot appropriate all the benefits flowing from the services their own taxes support—they pay taxes which unavoidably benefit others in the same metropolitan areas. This being the case, they are reluctant to pay higher taxes for improved services; instead, they will prefer to utilize their incomes for objects of private consumption, whose benefits are almost entirely appropriable by individual consumers.

The undernourishment also reflects the disparate distribution of tax bases and fiscal needs among jurisdictions. Poorer jurisdictions either simply do not have the taxable resources to finance more adequate levels of service, or, if they have disproportionately large needs (for services connected with poverty, for example), fear that the differentially heavy tax rates needed to finance the needs will stir migration of businesses and affluent residents, thus further weakening their tax bases. And the richer jurisdictions, no matter how altruistic their residents may be, do not have the authority to tax themselves to provide services in neighboring poor jurisdictions.

To a limited extent, fragmentation and local tax support do provide an incentive for higher expenditure levels, as in the case of the very high income suburb which is in effect a private club, providing superior services to its affluent members. But this is extremely limited, and the general rule is rather the opposite.

The Location of Economic Activity. In general, a tax imposed to raise revenue—and its revenue productivity is surely by far the strongest argument for the property tax—is best if it tends to be neutral in its impact on the choices of individuals and businesses: choices among alternative forms of consumption, types of productive inputs, and geographic locations. The property tax is decidedly *unneutral* in all these respects, but the really important unneutrality concerns the location of economic activity. The most important aspect of this locational influence is connected with the economic future of the large central city. The usually high effective rates on business property in the central cities do add to their relative unattractiveness as a site for industrial investment.[3] And, heavy taxation of investment in housing is unquestionably a deterrent to the needed replacement of much of the housing stock of the nation's older cities.

Housing in Central Cities. The property tax on housing by and large is borne by the occupants of taxable housing (except for that part of the tax which is on the land underlying rented housing) and, as such, is equivalent in character to an excise tax on actual and imputed housing expenditure. For the country as a whole, the property tax on housing works out to be similar to an excise tax of approximately 20 per cent on housing expenditures. This is *far higher* than ordinary American taxes on other forms of consumer expenditure (with the usual exceptions of liquor, tobacco, and gasoline). Moreover, in the larger urban areas, especially those outside the South, the excise tax rate is much higher—25, 30, or even 35 per cent.[4]

[3] In regard to investment in office buildings, even higher central city taxes seldom are a deterrent, since the location rents stemming from central city locations for office activities usually far exceed property tax differentials.

[4] In New York City as of 1960, the median value for real estate tax payments as a percentage of cash housing costs (of homeowners) or rental receipts, excluding the tax payments, was about 33 per cent. See Graduate School of Public Administration, New York University, *Financing Government in New York City*, 59–60, 703–705.

Housing taxes are therefore sharply unneutral with regard to consumption choices and should tend to discourage the consumption of housing. This is *not* likely to occur in relatively homogeneous suburban communities where the property tax on housing is probably most often viewed as a kind of charge for public services, particularly schools. That is, the consumer simultaneously buys, within his total expenditures for housing (including property taxes), a package which includes housing, neighborhood amenities, and public services. The benefits associated with the payment of taxes substantially dilute the deterrent effect on housing expenditure.

This, however, is hardly the case in large central cities where the association between payment of taxes and benefits from public services is tenuous indeed for any individual taxpayer. The individual consumer observes that housing, including property taxes, is expensive. It is likely that an effective strategy for city rebuilding requires that central city housing be relatively cheap, not relatively expensive.

Other Effects on Metropolitan Development. The property tax, therefore, works against the central city with regard to investment in housing and in industrial plants (and equipment, in the majority of states where this is taxed). The effect is aggravated because central cities so often must finance redistributive services and other services of a metropolitan-areawide character from property tax revenues.

But it also has an effect on development patterns beyond the central city. In some parts of the country, especially those characterized by a multiplicity of small jurisdictions, it has encouraged land use controls designed to minimize public service costs and maximize tax base within each small jurisdiction. That is, communities try to zone in nonresidential property and expensive housing and zone out moderately priced housing, the former with a highly favorable ratio of tax base to service needs and the latter with a highly unfavorable ratio. Unquestionably, this leads to less than optimal land use, with greatly increased transport costs.

The Persistence of the Property Tax

Any tax, however defective, is a good deal less objectionable if imposed at low and stable rates than if it is utilized at high and rising rates. The latter is the situation with regard to the property tax. Collections amount to roughly 3.5 per cent of gross national product currently, compared to about 2.5 per cent twenty years ago. Effective rates averaged about 1.0 per cent of GNP in the earlier period, and are now about 1.5 per cent.

As recently as a decade ago, it was feasible to predict that the property tax would decline greatly in importance in future years. State governments were increasingly adopting sales taxes and expanding state school aid programs, thus lessening reliance on the property tax to finance the most costly of property-tax-financed services, the public schools. Local government use of non-property taxes appeared to be spreading rapidly.

It is now quite apparent that, despite its many defects and despite the earlier expectations, the property tax is not about to wither away. As a percentage of total state-local tax revenue, the property tax has been stable, in a 44 to 46 per cent range, since 1950. This relative stability is a nationwide phenomenon. However, there have been some interesting regional differences. In the northeastern and Great Lakes states which have traditionally relied heavily upon it, the property tax has declined slightly in relative importance in the past decade. But in the southern states, which traditionally have relied much less heavily on the property tax, there actually has been a small increase in its importance.

This development seems clearly associated with the trend toward urbanization. Property tax revenues in most southern metropolitan areas have recently risen greatly—in the Memphis area, for example, from 1957 to 1966 the increase was 173 per cent. As urbanization continues, local government expenditure rises rapidly, as does the visible base of taxable real property. The property tax, being the residual source of local government funds, quite naturally rises in relative importance under such conditions.

93

Therefore, despite the recent adoption of major non-property taxes in such bastions of the property tax as New Jersey, Nebraska, and Massachusetts, it is a reasonable guess that the property tax will continue to provide at least 40 per cent of rapidly rising state-local tax revenue over the next decade, if present trends continue. This implies rising effective property tax rates and a situation in which the defects become steadily more onerous.

Minimizing the Defects

All this is essentially a consequence of the great pressure on state-local government fiscal resources, which appears to preclude any significant de-emphasis of the property tax. Even if the funds necessary to reduce the budgetary responsibilities of the property tax are simply not available (and the point of this paper, reserved for the moment, is that this supposition need not be true), there are ways to minimize some of the defects. But these are not likely to be adopted widely.

For example, property tax disparities within metropolitan areas could be reduced by structural reform of local government that is designed to reduce the extent of fragmentation or to provide a wider geographic net for property tax levies. There are a number of ways in which this could be done. For example, the role of county government (outside the South) could be enhanced by giving the county more functions, thereby levying a larger fraction of the property tax on a uniform county-wide basis. Or, as has been suggested in a number of places, some type of fiscal federation might be arranged within metropolitan areas, such as an areawide tax levy for an area foundation school program in addition to the state foundation programs, thereby reducing school tax rate disparities to minor proportions. Any reform which results in a larger proportion of the total property tax levy being imposed on a uniform basis will reduce both tax rate disparities and the interjurisdictional regressivity of the property tax.

This hardly seems likely to prove a very popular course of action. It amounts to asking (or requiring) the presently tax-favored jurisdictions to surrender their advantages and permit themselves to be more heavily taxed in behalf of their less fortunate neighbors. It is difficult indeed to present this to the potential losers as anything more than unrequited philanthropy.

A second approach might be radical reform of the property tax itself to eliminate the present locational unneutralities and the present deterrent effects on investment in housing. This would be the consequence of converting the existing tax into one which rests much more heavily on site values and much less heavily on buildings and equipment.

The argument for exclusive taxation of site values, or for substantially heavier taxation of land than of buildings, is an old one; differential site value taxation is widely practiced—in western Canada, Australia, New Zealand, and South Africa, for example. The merits of the case have been submerged for many years by the extravagant claims of the proponents of site value taxation. Moreover, skepticism has been bolstered by the apparent absence of discernible effects in the places where site valuation is utilized.

However, the case for site value taxation is a good one. The argument, on equity grounds, is that most of the value of land is a consequence, not of actions by individual owners, but of collective investment, community development, and population growth. Individual landowners therefore can realize large "unearned increments" over a period of time. It is entirely appropriate for the community to recapture these unearned increments by taxation and use them for community purposes. There are complications in this equity argument, related to the fact that most landowners have already paid, in their purchase prices, for at least some of the unearned increment, but by and large the equity argument makes sense.

The economic argument is even more compelling. A tax on site value which is independent of the improvements on the site will not affect entrepreneurial decisions as to the use of the site: the best (most profitable) use of the site before tax will remain the best after the tax is imposed. In other words, the tax is neutral

95

with regard to land use decisions. Since the present property tax, on both land and improvements, is *not* neutral but tends to discourage investment in buildings, a switch to exclusive (or differentially heavy) site value taxation would tend to have strong land use effects.

Provided that demand permits, it would encourage owners to develop their sites more intensively, in an effort to minimize tax liability as a percentage of current receipts, since additional investment in buildings would not increase tax liability. Within individual urban jurisdictions, taxes on vacant land would tend to rise, thereby increasing the cost of holding vacant land and making the speculative withholding of it from development a less attractive proposition. Thus, a switch to site value taxation would be likely to have its maximum impact in two parts of a metropolitan area—in the central sections, where it would encourage more investment in buildings, and in the outlying sections, where it would tend to discourage land speculation and the resulting discontinuous patterns of land development (less "leapfrogging" over sites withheld from the market).

In theory, there are few if any legitimate economic arguments against site value taxation. On an operational level, there are grounds for hesitation. First of all, one may doubt the actual strength of the positive tendencies associated with a switch to site value taxation. It is, after all, a major institutional change, and major institutional changes should not be pressed unless their positive effects are also expected to be major in extent. However, it should be noted that effective property tax rates in most American metropolitan areas are high and rising. The negative land use effects of the present tax are likely to become more apparent in time, and the likely benefits from a change in the basis of taxation will increase correspondingly.

Second, there is some question about the revenue adequacy of site value taxation. Some calculations suggest that the present yield of property taxes on nonfarm realty substantially exceeds the total rental value of privately owned nonfarm land. Thus, even a 100 per cent site value tax might not yield enough to fully replace the existing property tax (on real property, exclusive of personalty). This suggests that only a partial, rather than a complete, shift is possible, diluting the possible advantageous land use effects.

Third, there are administrative problems. But the very existence of site value taxation over a lengthy period in other advanced countries suggests that these problems are not insuperable. In fact, some people claim that exclusive site value taxation makes the valuation process a good deal easier than it is under the more conventional system of taxing both land and buildings. I suspect that this is not so, if equivalent standards of quality are applied, if only because there are fewer market sales of unimproved sites than of improved sites to use as a test of assessment quality.

However this may be, surely the most difficult system of all to administer is one in which both land and buildings are taxed, but at differential rates. This makes it very important to accurately value land and buildings *separately*. Under a pure system of site value taxation, the building value is irrelevant. Under the conventional property tax, the distinction between land and building for any individual site is also irrelevant, although the statutes may require the assessor to make some statement about the notional separation. Differential taxation is feasible in both practice and concept, but it is by no means easy.

Thus the verdict here on site value taxation is a favorable one. But it is a radical reform indeed. An examination of the long history of the property tax in the United States produces much skepticism about the likelihood of this or any other radical reform. After all, it has proven very difficult to achieve even a modicum of administrative reform, despite constant efforts, and this is hardly radical in nature.

Financing the Redistributive Services

An equally strong intellectual case, and a far more promising political one, can be made for relieving the property tax from the job of financing *all* services linked to the existence of poverty.

During the last thirty years, each of the important institutional changes which reduced pressures on the property tax has been associated with redistributive services. These include the federal and state assumption of most public welfare costs in the thirties via grants-in-aid, transfers of functional responsibilities, or direct federal social insurance programs; the steady expansion of the role of the state government in financing education in the past twenty years; the gradual increase in federal financing of health services (either directly or through grants-in-aid), culminating in Medicare and the 1965 Social Security amendments; the federal role in providing housing for low-income people; and most recently, the new federal participation in anti-poverty programs and in the costs of education where there are extensive pockets of poverty. All of this in combination has not been sufficient to keep effective property tax rates from rising at a fairly rapid rate. But without external aid to urban-area local governments, the increase might have been far more rapid.

There is, by now, sufficient interdependence to call for the virtual elimination of local property tax support of *all* poverty-linked public services, including public assistance costs (one sixth of which is now financed from local sources), other public welfare costs, health and hospital services for the poor, and the extra costs of local educational programs aimed essentially at the poor and disadvantaged. At present, local tax-supported expenditures for poverty-linked services equal at least 10 per cent of total property tax revenues on a nationwide basis and substantially more for the large central cities. Increased federal and state aid sufficient to eliminate this would make the property tax a more rational instrument of national public policy (by reducing its contradictory income-distribution role) and, at the same time, would reduce the adverse impact of the property tax on new investment in central cities.

Sharing Federal Revenues

In view of the monetary pressures confronted by state governments—the need to support all sorts of costly public services other than those linked to poverty—the prospects for a greater state government role in financing the poverty-linked services are not promising. This, then, is an appeal for more federal money, either in the form of expanded grants-in-aid or in the form of expanded direct federal programs—for example, the conversion of public assistance into a new and improved direct federal income maintenance program. The prospects for this, after Viet Nam, seem promising.

The value of such steps is considerable but this would not de-emphasize the property tax enough, nor would it correct the basic fiscal imbalance in our federal system of government. Simply stated, the imbalance is this. The federal government employs highly productive and buoyant revenue sources, and income rises annually (in periods of full employment) by $8 billion. The principal source, the individual income tax, scores rather well when measured by all the canons of taxation. But the federal government has a limited, marginal responsibility for the provision of civilian public services, especially those of great significance in urban areas.

In contrast, state and local governments have far less buoyant revenue sources, and some—like the property tax—are burdened with serious defects. Moreover, they are seriously inhibited in the use of the taxing powers they legally possess by the fear (whether merited or not) of the potentially adverse economic consequences of differentially high levels of taxation. And they do have the principal responsibility for the provision of civilian public services in a society with high and rising aspirations for improved public services.

Looking beyond the Viet Nam War, the likely consequences of the fiscal imbalance are continued increases in state-local tax rates, including the property tax (as the residual financing for urban services), while the superior federal taxes are repeatedly reduced. The latter is likely *even if* there is huge expansion in the federal role in providing poverty-linked services. A quadrupling of federal spending for the purposes now served by public assistance (including Medicaid), anti-poverty, and related programs would cost an additional $20 billion. This sounds huge, but it is equal to the federal revenue *increase* which accrues in only two and one-half years.

One conceivable resolution might be new and expanded federal grants for specific state-local programs. But there are a vast number of such grants now, many recently enacted, and a real resistance to further proliferation. One reason for this resistance surely is the implicit realization that there is a very limited nationwide interest in the performance of the many specific state-local government activities and that the spillovers of costs and benefits among the states are limited, however great the spillovers may be among adjacent communities within individual metropolitan areas. There is an obvious national interest in the eradication and alleviation of poverty and an equally obvious national interest in improving the educational preparation of a highly mobile population. There are some public problems which involve technological interstate spillovers, like the pollution of interstate waters, but the actual and potential public costs of dealing with such problems are really not very great. The case for federal aid in situations other than these is hard to discern, and the success of past appeals for the relatively modest grants involved (*e.g.*, for mass transportation) seems essentially attributable to log-rolling.

But there is an obvious national interest in having healthy and well-financed state and local governments providing a wide range of services. This, in the light of the fiscal imbalance, argues for a system of general-purpose, or unconditional, federal grants. The most widely discussed program for distributing such grants is the Heller-Pechman plan[5] which provides principally for per capita grants to the states. The plan would distribute a total which is equal to a specified fraction of the individual income tax base, a base which increases rapidly as the economy expands. This pro-

[5] See Joseph A. Pechman, "Financing State and Local Government," American Bankers Association, *Proceedings of a Symposium on Federal Taxation* (1965), 71–84.

posal would impose few limitations on the uses to which the states could put the new funds.

The advantages of a plan along these lines lie in its simplicity and sureness. If the fiscal imbalance is of major proportions, it is important to develop a mechanism which will transfer large and growing volumes of federal funds and will do so with some assurance. The Heller-Pechman plan does this, since the funds provided will rise automatically as the economy grows. If the total distribution is set at a fixed percentage of the individual income tax base, it will come close to doubling in the next decade, without further action by Congress.

This proposal recognizes the great diversity in needs for public services throughout the country, permitting the states to establish their own sets of priorities. Moreover, the plan recognizes that the distribution of responsibilities between the states and their local units varies greatly among the states. There is no simple way to transmit federal funds directly to the governmental units actually providing the services since in some states like New York the state government provides only minimal services directly through its own agencies, while in others, like Hawaii, the state government functions almost as a city government. The Heller-Pechman plan therefore leaves the distribution of new federal funds to the states for their own decision-making.

Opponents view the simplicity and flexibility of the plan as major defects, not virtues. They argue that there is no assurance that the funds will be used for high-priority purposes and even less assurance that the states will recognize the needs of their local units. This apprehension seems very much misplaced. State governments have used the increased revenue from their own taxes over the past twenty years to greatly increase aids to local governments, to improve higher education, and to further health and welfare activities.

In essence, the opponents of general-purpose federal grants distrust state government *per se*, even after reapportionment. It is difficult to share this distrust. Indeed, in this stage of our national development, with most states heavily urban in character, the state governments are the best substitutes for metropolitan government we have or are likely to get.

An additional criticism of proposals for general-purpose federal grants is that there is no way to make certain that the states will use the funds to finance additional public services. Instead, the new federal money might be used to support other programs which should be paid for by increased state and local taxation.

I view this as an advantage, rather than a disadvantage, since the property tax will be by far the most important of the state-local tax rates whose rise is slowed by the availability of large increments of federal money. In short, my conclusion is that federal tax sharing is a sound and necessary innovation in American fiscal federalism, and would be even if the property tax were a far better revenue instrument than it is. The case is greatly strengthened by the fact that federal tax sharing affords one of the few really effective means of de-emphasizing the property tax over the remainder of this century.

WAYS THE FEDERAL GOVERNMENT MAY STRENGTHEN STATE AND LOCAL FINANCING

JOHN SHANNON

ANALYSIS OF THE VARIOUS MEANS by which the national government may aid state and local governments requires consideration of both the tax and expenditure possibilities. With respect to expenditures, it frequently is suggested that the national government should permit state and local governments greater budgetary leeway by placing heavier emphasis on the more general forms of grants-in-aid and less on the present types of narrow categorical aid programs. With respect to taxes, it has been argued that the national government should abandon its traditional hands-off policy in favor of a positive approach to encourage states to create a more effective and equitable tax system via such tax coordination techniques as positive and negative tax credits.

In addition, there are a number of indirect methods by which the national government could aid state and local governments. For example, a general tax reduction might be viewed as an indirect aid to state and local governments since this would free revenue for state and local tax purposes and, if properly timed, would spur the economy. Similarly, the adoption of a guaranteed family income plan would relieve state and local governments of a considerable portion of their present welfare burden and improve their ability to handle other problems. However, our concern is with the more direct approaches to the problem.

Diversification of Our Grant System

The extraordinary expansion of our present grant-in-aid system stands out as the most significant recent development in intergovernmental fiscal relationships. Federal aid to state and local governments has increased from approximately $3 billion in 1955 to an estimated $17 billion for the fiscal year 1968. During this period federal aid as a percentage of total state and local revenue grew from 10 per cent to 17 per cent. This dramatic expansion is also reflected in the proliferation of major grant programs: there were forty-four in 1955 and approximately ninety-five for the fiscal year 1968. A detailed count reveals more than 400 subprograms and specific grant authorizations, with 128 in the educational field alone.

The rapid, uncoordinated, piecemeal expansion of the federal grant system has created major administrative problems. Programs with similar objectives are, for various reasons, administered by differing agencies, e.g., in the field of water pollution study four separate agencies administer different grant programs, each of which has different specific qualifications and requirements and different allocation and matching provisions. Such excessive categorization produces rigidities that limit state and local discretion in the administration of programs. Until recently, the categorical health grants were a striking illustration of such rigidity. A recent congressional committee found that there were sixteen different formulae and project grants covering cancer, chronic illness, dental disease, heart disease, mental illness, mental retardation, tuberculosis, venereal disease, neurological diseases, general health services, radiological help, some health services, and schools of public health. The committee also discovered that funds appropriated for each of these specific categories could not be transferred to any other category and could not be used to combat other public health problems, not even those which represented a more serious threat to health. With the enactment of the Partnership in Health Act of 1966 (P.L. 89–749), a major breakthrough was achieved wherein the sixteen categories were combined in one program. This will at least give state health agencies a better opportunity to shift funds and direct priorities along lines that seem most important to state and local authorities.

Expediting Grant Consolidations

The Advisory Commission on Intergovernmental Relations supports a new plan for speeding up the consolidation of federal grant programs. Specifically, the commission has endorsed Title VI of Senator Edmund Muskie's bill on intergovernmental cooperation (Senate Bill 698). This measure would authorize the President to submit grant consolidation plans to Congress by a procedure similar to the one used for administrative reorganization proposals—plans that would consolidate individual grant programs within the same general functional area, fix administrative responsibility in one department, and specify the formula to be used in allocating funds for the program. Then, unless the House or Senate should indicate their disfavor by means of a resolution, the President's plan would become effective ninety days after its submission to Congress. Bills incorporating this proposal have been introduced by both parties, insuring bipartisan support. The President, however, has not yet given his blessing.

The logic underlying the commission's support of this approach rests on the belief that the "presidential initiative-congressional veto" approach to grant consolidation stands out as the most effective way to achieve rapid grant consolidation. At the same time, the plan preserves the discretion of Congress, provides adequate opportunity for formal hearings, and allows a reasonable period for debate and voting.

Heller-Type Aid

While consolidation of federal grants would provide greater leeway for state and local policy-makers as well as for federal cabinet officers, it falls short of meeting the demands of those who urge increased aid to state and local governments on a "no strings attached basis"—a teletype plan. The basic justification for this type of aid is found in the contention that the federal government has superior fiscal resources while state and local governments are the ones confronted with mounting expenditure requirements. Thus, the advocates of revenue or tax sharing urge the national government to provide a limited degree of general aid to financially hard pressed state and local governments as soon as our military requirements subside. This, of course, assumes

that after Viet Nam is behind us the national revenue will produce surpluses in which state and local governments could share.

This approach to revenue sharing has important intergovernmental fiscal ramifications. First, there is a basic organizational
problem. Is it appropriate to divorce tax and expenditure responsibilities? If we adopt a hedonistic pleasure-pain calculus as the
basis for our fiscal operations, the person who endures the pain
of raising revenue should have the pleasure of saying how it should
be spent. Second, there is the practical problem of how the federal government will apportion the "no strings attached money"
between the state and local governments. Since the commission
has this policy issue on its agenda, I am not in a position to take
sides. The point can be made, however, that we are moving toward
a more generalized system of federal aid instead of the problem-
by-problem approach. The pendulum is obviously swinging toward consolidating grants within broader functional areas. There
is increasing evidence that more attention will be directed to improving intergovernmental relationships and less toward solving
narrow functional problems at the federal level.

Heightened sophistication in terms of intergovernmental relationships, however, will not eliminate the basic tension that will
arise when dollars are transferred from the national treasury to
state and local governments. The policy-makers at the federal
level will be under continuing and heavy pressure to set some
standards or tie some strings to the money transferred to state and
local government. We are not going to completely eradicate the
pleasure-pain calculus. By the same token, state and local policy-
makers will continue to demand as much budgetary leeway as
they think they can get. Thus, the problem of reconciling national
expenditure objectives with the diverse needs of state and local
governments will not go away. About the best we can hope for
is a more even balancing of these conflicting forces.

Strengthening the State and Local Tax System
It can be argued that much of the current rustling in the intergovernmental cathedral is traceable to an imbalance of fiscal

policy at the federal level. Specifically, the federal government has been too quick to prescribe detailed expenditure policies for state and local governments in connection with their aid programs and too slow in helping state and local governments create more efficient and equitable tax systems. The reason is obvious. From a political standpoint, it is hazardous to tell state and local governments how to raise their tax revenues as well as how to spend them. Attempts on the part of Congress to use tax credits as a device for encouraging state governments to adopt income taxes is often denounced as an outrageous intrusion into the sovereign area of state government. At a result, Congress has been urged to pursue a policy of neutrality between state and local use of income, sales, and property taxes. The business community is especially concerned about an emphasis on neutrality.

One significant departure from the neutrality principle occurred in the 1920's when Congress authorized the payment of state inheritance taxes as a partial credit against the federal estate tax. This action was taken at a time when Congress and the state governments were competing in the area of death taxes, and the grant of a tax credit by the federal government helped to stabilize the state inheritance tax. The Advisory Commission has taken a rather strong position on the matter of federal tax credits. In 1961, it recommended that Congress increase the credit allowable for state inheritance tax in order to provide more revenue for state and local governments. The commission qualified its recommendation with the stipulation that the increased credit be granted only if the state moves from an "inheritance base" to an "estate base" and only if the state provides assurance that the effect of increased credit will redound to the benefit of the state treasury rather than to individual federal taxpayers.[1]

More recently, the Advisory Commission has advocated preferential tax treatment for state and local income tax payments.[2] The commission based its recommendation for a partial credit

[1] Advisory Commission on Intergovernmental Relations, *Coordination of State and Federal Inheritance, Estate, and Gift Taxes*, January, 1961.

[2] Advisory Commission on Intergovernmental Relations, *Federal-State Coordination of Personal Income Taxes*, October, 1965.

107

on the finding that the so-called neutrality policy now pursued by the federal government is more apparent than real, *i.e.*, the intensive federal use of the income tax has in fact forced state policy-makers into using the sales tax. State legislators argue that the federal government has so pre-empted the income tax field that they have no alternative but to make more use of the consumer levels. As a consequence, the commission stated, it is necessary to give the state income tax a limited degree of preferential treatment on the federal tax return in order to balance the tax policy scales.

Admittedly, the science of public finance is not sufficiently exact to provide the precise amount of inducement that will compensate for the deterrent effect of heavy federal taxes. Reasonable inferences, however, can be drawn from historical experience. Clearly, a 90 to 100 per cent credit would tip the scales in favor of personal income taxation. No state could refrain from financing most of its needs by writing drafts on the U.S. Treasury. It is equally clear that the present deductibility system makes inadequate compensation for the high federal rates and that, as a consequence, federal policy tips the scales in favor of consumer consumption taxation. This suggests that a 40 per cent credit would come closer to steering a middle course between under- and overcompensation.

As might be expected, the Advisory Commission's middle-of-the-road proposal has drawn fire from both sides. Critics on the right contend that this limited degree of preferential federal tax treatment for state personal income taxes violates neutrality. Critics on the left suggest that a larger credit, 80–100 per cent, would give rise to nationwide adoption of income tax. In essence, it is felt that a move to strike at the doctrine of state tax sovereignty should strike to kill.

Although there is disagreement as to the amount of preference, there is substantial agreement that a greater use of the personal income tax by state governments would facilitate the solution of two critical problems. First, it would provide states a revenue source with growth potential. State and local expenditures now tend to multiply at a faster rate than revenues. Consequently, the states need a source that has a high growth potential. Second, state income taxes would lessen the impact of the sales and property taxes on low-income groups. In reality, a personal income tax at the state level would combat regressivity in two ways: (1) it would lessen the need for sales and property tax dollars, and (2) it would prevent a regressive situation from getting worse.

A far more promising method for combating regressivity is the transformation approach—a system of positive and negative state income tax credits for state sales and local property tax payments. This would tend to make sales and property taxes conform more closely to the ability-to-pay principle. Such tax credit has existed in limited form since 1963—Indiana was the first state to adopt such a plan in 1963. During World War II Congress considered such tax credits when it anticipated the necessity of a national sales tax. Since 1963, Colorado, Hawaii, and Massachusetts have adopted the positive and negative tax credit device. These plans permit an allowance (credit) of state sales tax against state income tax. If a taxpayer has no state income tax liability, he will merely file an income statement and the state tax department will send a check for the amount of the sales tax paid—negative tax credit is equated with a cash refund. The most significant application of such a credit system occurred in 1964, when Wisconsin adopted the positive and negative tax credit in an effort to reduce residential tax burdens borne by low-income, elderly householders. The Wisconsin legislature took the position that if an elderly householder had a property tax burden of more than 5 per cent of his total household, he was entitled to tax relief. The legislature declared that the amount in excess of 5 per cent should be claimed by the property owner as a positive credit against his state income tax. In the case where no income tax was due a negative credit situation existed and a cash refund was in order.

There are several points to be noted: (1) the credit is admin-

istered by the state income tax department, not a welfare department; (2) it is the state treasury that reimburses the taxpayer,
not the local government; and (3) it is assumed that 25 per cent
of the rental paid by tenants is imputed residential property tax.

This transformation effect via the positive and negative tax
credit route stands out as a promising recent development in the
field of tax coordination. Through the positive and negative tax
credit, it is possible to convert regressive levies into proportional
or even into progressive taxes. It is only a question of time before
the federal government will profit from the Wisconsin experiment. That is, pressure will be placed on Congress to use this
approach to aid persons carrying excessive state and local tax
burdens in relation to their income. In fact, recently Congressman Herbert Tenzer from New York introduced a bill that had
some characteristics of the Wisconsin plan. It provided tax credit
relief to federal income tax payers for that amount of their local
property tax in excess of 5 per cent of their net taxable income.

The interest of federalism might be better served if states are
encouraged to assume this "circuit breaker" role to prevent tax
overloads. For example, the cost incurred by states when aiding
persons and families carrying excessive tax loads could be borne
partially by the federal government. This "circuit breaker" approach rests on the belief that an affluent society should be able
to finance most of its domestic public services without taxing
low-income families or centralizing a high degree of decision-
making responsibility at the national government level. The emphasis is upon the individual's total tax situation.

Summary

The growing demand for a reform in federal aid will probably
have two major fiscal impacts. The expenditure side will em-
phasize a broad form of grant program with less emphasis on the
narrower categorical approach. Whether this trend will embrace
an unconditional fund is an open question to be resolved politically. It should be emphasized, however, that most federal grant

money will continue to have strings. The emphasis on a broader grants system should give state and local policy-makers greater budgetary leeway. On the receipt side attention will be given to strengthening the tax system. Through a judicious use of positive and negative tax credits designed to encourage states to remove the regressivity of their own tax system, Congress can make these systems more equitable and more accepted revenue instruments for state and local governments. It is becoming increasingly apparent that policy-makers must add a third dimension to their tax calculations. That is, fiscal policy should include the objectives of income redistribution, economic stabilization, and an accepted and equitable intergovernmental tax system.

FISCAL OUTLOOK FOR STATE AND LOCAL GOVERNMENT

Elsie M. Watters

THE PROBLEMS OF FINANCING local and state governments are complex and do not lend themselves to easy solution. Individual opinions vary as to how well these governments have met their responsibilities in the past, and there is no unanimity concerning the severity of their future problems in relation to those of the past. Recent research indicates a need to re-examine the old "pessimism" with which state and local finance has been viewed. Local governments exist only as entities created by the various fifty states; consequently, no uniform rules have been set up from one state to another with respect to the division of authority for taxing and spending between state and local governments. Considering the nation as a whole, the states turn over 34.4 per cent of their general revenues to local governments. These percentages, however, are highly variable among the states.

This paper deals with projections of general expenditures of state and local governments through the year 1975. No attempt is made to relate these projections separately to the local level—state and local governments are treated jointly. The main body of the paper is concerned with a study prepared by the Tax Foundation, the results of which were released in November, 1966.

The Tax Foundation Study

Since 1960 state and local government finances have been discussed in much detail, and it has become increasingly clear that this subject is rapidly developing into a national problem. Until recently, however, there have been few studies devoted to the long-range outlook for state and local expenditures. The last projections of the Tax Foundation, made in 1955, pointed up our lack of knowledge about state and local finance problems. These projections did not foresee even vaguely the large growth in service expenditures by state and local governments that occurred during the first half of the 1960's.

The recent research was designed to project, under specified assumptions, the levels of services which state and local governments would be called upon to supply by 1970 and 1975, the potential revenues from all sources (calculated by using 1965 tax rates), and the probable magnitude of debt financing and associated financing requirements.[1] Recognizing that state and local governmental fiscal activities are interrelated in many significant ways with the total economy, the study was based on an over-all model which took into account national production, population, labor force, employment, length of workweek, total man-hours, productivity, and prices. Different arrangements of these variables can lead to a virtually endless array of possible levels of activity. Since there is no probability model which can produce maximum likelihood estimates of the relevant parameters, the elements of the economic model were necessarily chosen on the basis of a preconceived hypothesis, and the over-all results reflect this judgment.

Although our evaluation of the specific elements of the model differs from the recently published evaluations of other models, there is remarkable agreement about the generated levels of gross national product. The Tax Foundation projections foresee the gross national product's rising in terms of current dollars from $681 billion in 1965 to $902 billion in 1970 and to $1,178 billion in 1975. For the entire ten-year period, the annual growth in GNP would be about 4 per cent in real terms and 1.6 per cent in prices, *i.e.*, 5.6 per cent per year, based on the money value of the dollar. Previously, the annual growth rates were 5.8 per cent per year from 1948 to 1960 and 6.2 per cent from 1960 to 1965. The GNP levels estimated in other models, *e.g.*, the Joint Economic Committee's, indicate "potential" GNP levels for 1970

---

[1] The main study dealt with general expenditures and excluded utility functions, liquor store operations, and insurance trust financing; these latter activities, however, were included in the consideration of debt transactions and as expenditures to the extent that they require some funding or subsidy from general treasuries.

of between $920 and $950 billion and for 1975 of from $1,205 to $1,310 billion (current dollar values). In publishing these estimates, the committee stated: "The U.S. economy has a potential for a rate of economic growth between 4 and 4 1/2 percent per year between 1965 and 1975. This is between one-third and one-half above the rate prevailing in the first two-thirds of this century, and is substantially above the 3.5 percent prevailing over the 17 years from 1948 to 1965. . . ." [2] Thus, it is clear that the realization of the Tax Foundation economic projections, while dependent upon a moderately high rate of economic expansion and reasonable price stability, does not represent the full potential which appears reasonably achievable.

Against the backdrop of such an economic environment, the study then turns to an effort to derive estimates of the future expenditures of state and local jurisdictions and the availability of funds in support of these expenditures. Although the two sides of the coin—expenditure and revenue—are by no means independent of each other, there is no *a priori* ground for choosing the direction of causality. Do expenditures automatically rise at an equal pace with growing revenues? Do revenues rise because of pressures first exerted on expenditures? Partial answers to both questions are affirmative. There are, however, tempering elements in both cases, and unfortunately the knowledge that there is some causal link between the amount we have available to spend and the amount we do spend is not very useful as a pragmatic device.

The task of projecting state and local finances thus poses a

---

[2] U.S. *Economic Growth to 1975: Potentials and Problems*, study prepared for the Subcommittee on Economic Progress of the Joint Economic Committee (Joint Committee Print), 89th Congress, 2nd session (Washington, D.C.: Government Printing Office, 1966), 24. The range in the committee's estimates results from two sets of alternatives concerning real growth rate and prices: the lower estimate is based on a 4.5 per cent annual rate of growth for real GNP and 2.0 per cent annual price increase from 1966 through 1975; the lower is based on 4.0 per cent annual rate of growth for real GNP and 1.5 per cent annual price increase from 1966 through 1975. The Tax Foundation's projections are slightly below the lower range of the committee's estimates primarily because they were developed by using 1965 as a benchmark, a year in which price inflation was unusually rapid.

dilemma at the outset. Should the amount of tax and other funds which might become available be projected as a limiting value for future expenditures, or should expenditure levels be projected without regard to the manner in which they are to be financed? The approach adopted was to treat spending and revenues for the most part as being independent of each other.[3] Ultimate concern was with the gap which might emerge between the prospective levels of cash outflow and inflow. Juxtaposition of the projections derived for spending and income would then reveal the extent of inequality between the two and dictate the nature of recommendations or conclusions which might be put forth for future fiscal solutions.

Expenditures for each of the major functions of state and local government (education, highways, health and hospitals, and public welfare) were projected separately by building up estimates of caseloads, unit costs, and prices based primarily on legislation already in effect. In estimating tax revenues, an effort was made to determine the yield of existing tax systems in response to projected changes in the general economy. Other revenues (primarily user charges, fees, and federal grants-in-aid) were estimated by extrapolating the historical ratios of these receipts to projected expenditure levels for related functions.

Expenditure Projections

Expenditure projections were by far the most difficult to derive because the raw materials differed greatly in each functional category. Data provided by the Governments Division, Bureau of the Census, had to be supplemented and reconciled with information from other government agencies and private organizations.[4] For each of the four major functions which constitute 71

---

[3] The definitions and concepts of the Governments Division, Bureau of the Census, were adopted for the study because they alone provide a systematic framework in which functional components will be additive.

[4] As an example of the forest of confusion into which one must wander and somehow find enlightenment, the total of all government expenditures for public welfare as reported by the Bureau of the Census came to $6.4 billion in fiscal 1965. Under a definition adopted by the Social Security Administration, expenditures for social welfare under all public programs amounted to $77.7 billion in 1965—twelve times as much.

per cent of total state and local general outlays, detailed historical studies were made of the elements associated with change and the weight assignable to each.

The basic assumption in the projections was that caseloads would be determined by certain attributes of the population, especially age and income characteristics, in relation to some benchmark period. For example, in estimating the numbers eligible for living allowances under public assistance programs, it was assumed that the rates of participation in the eligible age classifications for the various categorical programs—old age assistance, aid to dependent children, etc.—would continue to change in a manner similar to the period 1960 to 1965 (with adjustment for program changes which affected eligibility). In this connection, it is interesting to note that the number of recipients of old age assistance per 1,000 persons aged 65 and over declined from 225 in 1950 to 118 in 1965; that the rate for persons in the aid for families of dependent children rose from 47 in 1950 to 62 in 1965; that recipients in the aid to the blind program declined from .9 to .8 in the same interim; and that general assistance declined from 6.2 to 3.8. There are, of course, many unseen factors which might account for these changes. For example, revisions of public policy which involve shifts among programs or changes in eligibility provisions could both explain the findings, at least in part.

In projecting future caseloads it was assumed that trends in these rates and the projected population in eligible age categories would determine the number of public assistance recipients in each category. The amounts each would receive was estimated by adjusting the 1965 expenditure for recent federal liberalization and by adding cost-of-living increments to future payments. The results indicated that the number of persons receiving public assistance living allowances would rise from around 7.6 million in 1965 to 9.2 million in 1975. Major shifts would be a decline in the old age category from 2.1 million to 1.8 million by 1975 and an increase in the dependent children category from 4.5

million to 6.0 million by 1975. Increasing payment allowances would tend to cause aid for the aged to remain at the $1.6 billion level. Increases, both in payments and number of persons, in the dependent children and disabled categories would raise the total from $4.0 billion in 1965 to $5.5 billion by 1975.

These are examples in which the age and income distribution of the population, employability, health, dependency, shifts in public policy, and other factors blend to produce what appear to be fairly predictable patterns. It might be added that the income effect, as represented by the upward shifting of the curve of real income distribution, which serves to lower the rate of participation in public assistance among eligible age groups has been offset by policy decisions and other factors which enable more persons to receive this type of aid. In the case of the aged, however, the income effect has been in evidence, as more and more of the elderly have been covered under social security. Reinforcing this trend has been a policy factor: shifts of cases from the Old Age Assistance category to Medical Assistance for the Aged, established in 1960, where more abundant government medical services are available.

Even though policy changes have occurred in the public assistance cash programs, such changes could be identified and incorporated into projections. However, problems arose with attempts to estimate the full effects of state and local programs of medical assistance under Title XIX of the 1965 Social Security Act Amendments. This legislation established new demands upon the states to provide comprehensive medical and health services to all members of the population who, though able to meet their regular living expenses, cannot provide full medical services for themselves and their families. Various deadlines for compliance with the federal provisions were established. The most important was that by 1975 the states must have made satisfactory progress toward providing such care for all medically indigent members of the population or lose all federal aid toward such care. Through this legislation, the federal government liberalized its own participation in medical payments under public assistance, but in turn it required far higher standards of service in the states coupled with increases in the number served.

No one is certain of what the eventual costs of this program will be to either the federal government or to the state and local governments. Spokesmen for the U.S. Department of Health, Education, and Welfare have stated that the program will eventually serve 35 million persons, or about one fifth of the nation's population. The Tax Foundation projections (assuming a continuation of the increase in the ratio of "poor and near poor" to total population that has occurred since 1950) estimated potentially eligible persons in 1975 at 31 million (under 65) and costs of $7 to $10 billion, depending upon the range of state services provided. An alternate estimate suggested that 49 million (one fourth of the population) under 65 might be covered, at a cost of $16 billion.

Education is the most expensive function of state and local governments, and it is second only to national defense in terms of all spending for general government. About 40 per cent of state and local outlays are for local public schools and colleges and universities. Moreover, a larger and larger share of the education dollar is being devoted to colleges and universities. The projections for education involved separate determinations for the major components—current expenditure versus capital outlay, local schools versus higher education, and a small miscellaneous category. Before developing an approach to the problem of making estimates of the fiscal needs of state and local government, it was necessary to examine the vast amount of research that has been conducted on the determinants of spending for education, especially at the local school level.[5] While highly in-

[5] We examined the projections of enrollments which had been recently prepared by the U.S. Office of Education and decided that, with the tools available to us, we could not improve on their results. These were carefully computed from past trends, taking into account age distribution of the population, increasing portions of students attending schools and colleges, the ratios of enrollments in public versus private institutions, and so on. We adjusted the local school pro-

structive, this proved to be a fruitless effort. The research was not directly useful in connection with our projections, and it is reported in the study only so that others may be spared similar pitfalls.

Outlook for State and Local Government Expenditures

The outlook for expenditures on the major state and local functions is highlighted by the estimate that all state and local expenditures are projected to rise from $75 billion in fiscal 1965 to $142 billion in 1975. This pattern represents continued high growth, but at a pace more nearly consistent with that of the first half of the 1960's than with the faster rate recorded in earlier postwar years. For the next decade, the indicated increase is 89 per cent, in comparison with a 122 per cent advance in the decade ending in 1965. The major factors contributing to this growth are as follows:

(1) Total state-local outlays for education are expected to reach $52.9 billion in 1975, an increase of 83 per cent over the current level of expenditure. This growth compares with a 144 per cent rise during the past decade. The relatively slower increase in expenditure is explained by an expected slow-down in enrollments in local schools between 1965 and 1970. From 1970–75 a diminution of some 1.2 million students is anticipated. For the decade, enrollment gains will average 162,000 per year. This compares to an average annual increase of 1,187,000 for the period 1955–65. If per-pupil standards continue to rise as they did in the first half of the 1960's, operating costs per pupil will reach $852 by 1975 (about 75 per cent higher than in 1965). Declining numbers of students will, however, restrain growth in expendi-

---

jections in accordance with later population projections which the Bureau of the Census had published and used the college enrollments projections without change. The capital outlay projections of the Office of Education were similarly treated. For current operating expenditures we again built in an improvement factor which projects changes in costs per enrollee according to rates experienced in the first half of the 1960's.

tures for operating as well as capital purposes. Local school spending is projected to approach $37.1 billion in 1975. This represents an increase of 66 per cent for the decade. During the decade 1955–65, spending for local schools rose 121 per cent.

Expenditures for institutions of higher education are projected to grow more rapidly than for public schools. Outlays are estimated to approximate $14.0 billion by 1975—an increase of 139 per cent above 1965. Current expenditures per full-time student are estimated to increase by about three fifths—from $1,593 in 1965 to $2,557 in 1975. While large increases in numbers enrolled will continue, it is significant to note that the greatest proportionate gain in college students (a 60 per cent increase in a five-year period) occurred in the first half of the 1960's. Enrollment gains are expected to rise by 45 per cent for the period 1965–70 and by 28 per cent for the period 1970–75.

(2) The second major addition to state and local government expenditures is in the area of public welfare. Total welfare outlays are expected to reach $17.1 billion in 1975—a 170 per cent increase from 1965. This projection reflects an assumed widespread response by states to the 1965 federal legislation in the field of medical care for the "medically indigent." This legislation calls for a shift of welfare expenditures (1) from financial aid for living support to payments for medical care; (2) from programs for the elderly to those for younger persons; and (3) from aid to the very poor to assistance to those with higher living standards. If these programs are implemented by state governments, medical costs under public assistance programs will rise by approximately $7.5 billion during the period 1965–75.

In the other major sector of public welfare—cash living allowances to the needy—only moderate rates of increase are indicated. This reflects an expected decline in the rate of growth of members of the population under 18 years old and over 65 years old. These two groups receive more welfare aid than others and have tended to increase more rapidly than other age categories during the postwar period. One other factor will probably check state and local welfare spending—the continued increase in the role of social insurance programs in the care of elderly persons.

(3) Future spending for health and hospitals is expected to rise by 97 per cent in the decade 1965–75—to a peak of $10.6 billion. Recent federal legislation affecting the over-all financing of national health services will indirectly influence the state-local health and hospitals sector; in particular, state-local hospitals may become more self-sustaining. These new programs will serve to reduce the role of state and local hospitals in the care of the poor who have health problems. While the over-all financial responsibility of state and localities for hospital and health services may decline in relation to the nation's total health expenditures, their administrative role in the broader field of health services, which include medical vendor payments under public welfare, seems likely to expand. Medical care costs and prices are expected to continue to mound rapidly.

(4) Highway outlays in 1975 are projected at $16.6 billion, 36 per cent above 1965. Land, construction, maintenance, and other highway costs have risen rapidly as a result of both price inflation and improvements in the quality of roads and streets. Such increases are estimated to continue at a similar pace throughout the projection period. The volume of highway construction, however, is projected to drop somewhat following the completion of the 41,000-mile interstate highway system. Future federal legislation will have an important bearing on actual highway outlays following the completion of the interstate highway system.

(5) The remaining services provided by the states and localities cover a wide range of activities. The total costs of these heterogeneous services are projected at approximately double their 1965 level.

Projections of Revenues and Over-All Finances

Given the initial decision to estimate future revenues from present tax systems, the problem of projection was less exacting in most instances than the task of estimating expenditures. Research on the elasticity of major sources of state tax revenue since 1959 provided a basis for determining tax yield as a function of income and the appropriate elasticity coefficients. The results indicated that tax revenues from the present system would increase from $52 billion in 1965 to some $90 billion in 1975. Other income to state and local governments, mainly associated with growing user charges (college tuition, hospital charges, etc.), was estimated as a function of expenditures involved. It is estimated that they will rise to $26.6 billion in 1975. This represents an increase of 127 per cent over the 1965 level.

The estimates of federal grants are to a large extent arbitrary because they were calculated on the basis of legislation already in effect.[6] According to some observers, the projections are lower than the levels which can reasonably be expected to result from existing programs. Actual amounts will depend in part upon domestic and international political factors not now foreseeable. For example, should the Great Society program be adopted and implemented in full, approximately $3 billion would be added annually to federal expenditures (largely grants-in-aid). This would be in addition to the built-in increases of similar size which automatically would occur under existing programs.[7] In this case, federal grants by 1975 would be in the neighborhood of $45 billion; some estimates run as high as $60 billion.[8]

General revenues from all sources are projected at $146.9 billion in 1975, an increase of 98 per cent for the decade. This estimate exceeds general expenditures in 1975 by approximately $5 billion. When allowance is made for broader financial operations

---

[6] One exception is the assumption that the federal government will extend its sharing under Title XIX programs for the medically indigent to all able-bodied persons aged 18 through 64.

[7] Gerhard Colm and Peter Wagner, *Federal Budget Projections* (Washington, D.C.: The Brookings Institution, 1966), 12.

[8] In hearings before the Senate Government Operations Committee's subcommittee on Intergovernmental Relations, Senator Edmund S. Muskie indicated that federal grants-in-aid are expected to reach $60 billion annually by 1975, four times the present figure. *Washington News*, Tax Foundation, November 25, 1966, p. 2.

of state and local governments (*e.g.*, borrowing and debt servicing, employee retirement, refunds on retirement), the over-all financial position is further strengthened, and a surplus of about $6.5 billion is indicated for 1975. If state and local governments continue to borrow approximately one-half the amount they spend for capital investment, total debt for all functions would rise from $100 billion in 1965 to $169 billion by 1975—an average of about $7 billion a year. This represents a decline in the relative growth rate of debt as well as a decline in the outstanding volume of net long-term debt in relation to revenues from state and local sources.

Summary

The estimated 89 per cent rise in public service outlays of state and local governments in the next decade would not only make allowance for automatic, built-in increases in service needs, but would also permit the same, or a slightly higher, rate of "improvement" in the level of services offered. For the past ten years, it was estimated that of the nearly 10 per cent annual growth in expenditures of these governments about 2 per cent represent "improvements" in the quality and scope of services. Whether this is an appropriate rate depends on the goals which are established for the public.

In conclusion, the findings summarized here suggest that the situation ahead is not quite so bleak as is commonly supposed. Although there is a reasonable prospect for some abatement in state and local financial problems, there are still many qualifications to the findings. The estimated results will not be achieved without careful planning, budgeting, and administration on the part of state and local governments.

PART FOUR

Special Financial Problems of State and Local Government

ECONOMIC CRITERIA FOR SOUND STATE DEBT FINANCING

WILLIAM D. ROSS AND JOSEPH M. BONIN

Introduction

T HE ELECTED OFFICIALS of state governments who must assume responsibility for state bond financing often have had no previous experience with debt financing. Since state borrowing is utilized somewhat infrequently in most states, and since the responsibility for borrowing is divided between several agencies and departments in many states, state officials have little opportunity to gain experience in planning and managing bond issues unless they possess an unusual measure of political longevity. If progress is to be made in debt management, those responsible for state borrowing must be prepared to learn from the experiences of others. This learning would be advanced if these experiences were formulated into principles and recommended practices which could be followed by officials responsible for state debt financing.

Unfortunately, not enough up-to-date and easily accessible information of this type is available to state officials. Municipal officials are more fortunate in having some useful debt management information made available to them through their Municipal Finance Officers Association.[1] Of course, many of the principles and practices of debt financing applicable to municipalities and other political subdivisions of states are also applicable at the state level. Nevertheless, the broad economic foundation, tax base, and fiscal powers of state governments would seem to justify separate consideration of state debt financing. A principal ob-

The essay is reprinted from the 1962 Proceedings of the Fifty-Fifth Annual Conference on Taxation, *National Tax Association (Harrisburg, Pa., 1963)*, 107–22.

[1] See David M. Ellinwood, Wade S. Smith, Walter H. Tyler, *et al.*, "Debt Management and Municipal Debt," *Municipal Finance*, XXIX (February, 1957), the entire issue; and, the two annual special issues of the *Daily Bond Buyer* prepared for the Municipal Finance Officers Association.

jective here is to direct attention to the need for perhaps greater differentiation between the criteria appropriate for judging state debt and the criteria for judging local debt financing.

The two facets of debt management are basic policy decisions and operational procedures. State debt policy decisions set the ground rules for state borrowing and may properly be codified in a state's constitution. They include debt limitation provisions and general provisions authorizing state borrowing. On the other hand, sound operational procedures require too much flexibility to be codified and thus should be left to state fiscal officers. These include decisions as to selling methods and debt retirement operations. Constitutional provisions governing state debt financing should ideally be limited in number and general in nature. They should not include details concerning "how to borrow" because these are operational procedures.

When to Borrow

Many studies that deal with state and local government borrowing begin by discussing "pay-as-you-go" and end by considering borrowing as something of a necessary evil. They rather apologetically state or imply that long-term borrowing should be reserved for financing various emergency activities and capital construction, if these things cannot be financed otherwise and if the public improvements are "self-supporting." [2]

State borrowing is more respectable than this and has greater justification. Borrowing can help a state in three ways: (1) it can finance public facilities essential to the proper functioning of the economy, (2) it can lead to a quickening of economic development, and (3) it can lead to a more equitable distribution of the costs of government services over time.

[2] For representative examples of conventional assumptions and attitudes about "pay-as-you-go," see C. W. Easter, "The Market for Municipal Bonds," *The Daily Bond Buyer*, Municipal Finance Association Special Issue, Pt. II (June 5, 1961), 21–23, 56; Virgil H. Hurless, "Obtaining Improvement Through Balanced Finance," *Municipal Finance*, XXVI (May, 1954), 138; Alex K. Hancock, "Value of Financial Planning," *Municipal Finance*, XXXIII (November, 1960), 75; Wade S. Smith, "Sound Financing for Sound Municipal Credit," *Municipal Finance*, XXIX (February, 1957), 122.

Physical facilities for education and medical care, highways, harbors, and other public improvements are essential to our economic system and must be provided in part by borrowing. It is a happy coincidence that public expenditures for these things are also growth stimulating. Borrowing may also contribute to greater equity for the taxpayer by deferring some of the costs of providing social goods to future users. The transfer of some financial costs to future users is accomplished by long-term borrowing. A current generation is not acting in its own interest if it assumes the entire burden of financing long-term improvements; and, certainly, it is not acting in the best interest of future generations if it pursues a narrow debt philosophy that so limits facilities and constrains economic development that future standards of living are depressed.

The borrowing by states which has taken place in this country appears to have occurred primarily because certain facilities were necessary, not because promises of greater economic growth and greater equity were significantly influential. In fact, judging from their current debts, it may be that the need for capital facilities has not been properly recognized in some states. In 1960, nine states had less than $15,000,000 each of total full-faith-and-credit and non-guaranteed debt outstanding, and seventeen states had less than $87,000,000 of total debt outstanding.[3]

<hr />

[3]

STATES WITH LESS THAN $87,000,000 OF TOTAL
DEBT OUTSTANDING, 1960

State	Amount*	State	Amount*
Alaska	$ 2,902,000	Vermont	$42,064,000
Nevada	4,027,000	Montana	49,017,000
South Dakota	6,261,000	New Mexico	50,741,000
Idaho	6,991,000	Iowa	53,902,000
Wyoming	8,733,000	Wisconsin	55,029,000
Arizona	12,442,000	Colorado	62,249,000
Nebraska	13,112,000	Missouri	85,436,000
North Dakota	14,370,000	New Hampshire	86,126,000
Utah	15,508,000	TOTAL:	$567,910,000

Source: Bureau of the Census, *Compendium of State Government Finance in 1960* (Washington, D.C.: Government Printing Office, 1961), 40–41.

* Includes full-faith-and-credit and nonguaranteed obligations of state toll facilities and institutions of higher education.

129

On the other hand, the ten states that have borrowed most heavily and account for 67 per cent of total American state debt[4] appear to have made their debt structures serve them well; the ratings given to their bonds are good and their credit reputations remain strong.[5] This is an indication that it is possible to borrow and still maintain a healthy credit standing if it is done properly.

In general, state constitutions should authorize full-faith-and-credit borrowing for essential public improvements and for the emergency purposes usually cited in state constitutions.

How Much to Borrow

After it has been determined that borrowing is permissible, the second major decision to be made is how much the state can borrow. The very limited use of borrowing in certain states is, of course, explained in some cases by severe constitutional limitations on state borrowing in terms of amounts, length of maturities, and borrowing procedures. In most cases these current provisions were imposed many years ago for reasons which have long since ceased to be relevant. Debt limits or referendum and procedural requirements either prohibit state borrowing or severely restrict it in some twenty states. "Only eight states can borrow freely at their own discretion." [6]

[4]

STATES WITH OVER $500,000,000 OF TOTAL
DEBT OUTSTANDING, 1960

State	Amount*	State	Amount*
New York	$2,791,472,000	Ohio	$908,876,000
California	2,087,942,000	Michigan	775,732,000
Pennsylvania	1,419,302,000	Connecticut	682,440,000
Massachusetts	1,265,363,000	Illinois	675,583,000
New Jersey	914,117,000	Maryland	584,125,000

TOTAL: $12,104,952,000 (out of total debt for all states of $18,127,909,000)

Source: Bureau of the Census, *Compendium of State Government Finance in 1960*, 40–41.
* Includes full-faith-and-credit and nonguaranteed obligations of state tool facilities and institutions of higher education.

[5] *Moody's Municipal and Government Manual* (New York: Moody's Investor Service, 1961), *passim*.

[6] Manuel Gottlieb, "The Revenue Bond and Public Debt," *Quarterly Review of Economics and Business*, II (May, 1962), 33.

Ratchford's approach to the question of debt limitations is still very pertinent today. In some states, borrowing can be left entirely to the legislative branch if that branch has proved itself responsible. In other states, constitutional debt limits may serve as safeguards to prevent abuse by an occasional irresponsible group that might gain control of the state government. In this case, some sort of limit is in order, but the limit should be a flexible one.[7]

Although the flexible type of limitation appears to be an obvious way of restricting borrowing, little use has been made of such debt limits. Only one very recent adoption of this type of plan, in Puerto Rico, may be cited:

> One of the most unique and tradition breaking actions in the debt limit field occurred in the *Commonwealth of Puerto Rico* where the voters approved a new constitutional amendment which expresses the debt limit in other than assessed valuations or a flat dollar amount. The new amendment provides that debt service in any fiscal year during the life of the bonds issued or guaranteed by the Commonwealth may not exceed 15% of the average annual revenues raised under Commonwealth legislation and covered into its treasury during the two preceding fiscal years. The step was taken to relate the debt limit to the wealth and income of the people and to their capacity to meet the debt as it comes due.[8]

Before the plan was initiated, Puerto Rico had a debt limit linked to the assessed valuation of property. This conventional technique has, unfortunately, tended to make general obligations appear to be secured only by particular revenues. Puerto Rico's new debt limit should be much more responsive to true changes in financial ability and should prove very sound.

State debt limitations should never be set up in terms of dollar amounts, assessment ratios, or duration of debt. If a constitutional limit must be specified, it should be made in terms of a ratio of

[7] B. U. Ratchford, *American State Debts* (Durham, N.C.: Duke University Press, 1941), 444–45, 592–97.

[8] Municipal Finance Officers Association, "Municipal Finance Newsletter," XXXVII (January 1, 1962), 2.

debt service charges to total state revenues in order not to bind future generations to the fiscal facts and practices of the past.[9]

Who Should Borrow

The third major policy decision which should be codified is the one which determines the agency or agencies of the state that will be delegated the responsibility for managing the state's debt.

The answer to the question of how many units should be permitted to carry out the state's borrowing should be based partly on considerations of specialization and scale. The state can hardly expect to do better than concentrate its debt management duties in a single specialized borrowing unit. Economies should result from better staffing, better planning, closer contact with the bond market, less distraction from other duties, and better debt reporting. Debt management is expensive, and in most states, the volume of borrowing is not large enough to justify the issuing of bonds by more than one or perhaps two state agencies.[10]

Responsibilities of the debt management agency should include (1) aiding other state agencies and the legislature with capital budgeting; (2) conferring with state agencies and the legislature about proposed debt legislation; (3) managing the sale, service, and retirement of bond issues; and (4) continuous and comprehensive reporting to the rating services, bond buyers, and the public of information about the state debt structure. The authority of a state's debt management agency ideally should be limited to the issuing and servicing of bonds and should never include responsibility for the expenditure of the proceeds of bond sales.[11]

[9] It might also be possible to establish limits relating debt to additional indicators of ability, such as personal income per capita. Some of the techniques of measuring tax burdens could be applied in formulating debt limits. For example, see Henry J. Frank, "Measuring State Tax Burdens," *National Tax Journal*, XII (June, 1959), 179–86.

[10] In Louisiana, state highway borrowing is on a sound basis already, so there would be no significant advantage in combining it with all other borrowing. William D. Ross and Joseph M. Bonin, "A Proposed New System of Non-Highway Bond Financing for Louisiana," *National Tax Journal*, XIII (December, 1960), 364–68.

[11] *Ibid.*, 367–68.

Of course, statutory changes would be required in every state in the nation to accomplish these objectives. In the meantime, states may minimize the inefficiencies of their bond financing machinery by avoiding the creation of new bond issuing authorities.[12]

Capital Budgeting

Although few states do, every state government should have a capital budget separate from its operating budget. The current operating expense budget should be financed on an annual basis from tax and other revenues. The capital budget, on the other hand, should include only capital improvement projects needed by the agencies of the state government which may not properly be included in the operating budget, and it should be projected forward for a period of five or more years.

The capital budget may include projects which can be financed on a pay-as-you-go basis, but it will also include projects which require long-term debt financing. Careful planning should go into the preparation of the capital expenditure budget and the development of a workable plan for financing the improvements needed. Small projects of a recurring type should normally be financed on a pay-as-you-go basis. Projects requiring very large expenditures at relatively infrequent intervals may properly be financed through borrowing in most cases. Projects of intermediate size usually require individual appraisal to determine the

[12] The state of Louisiana represents an unenviable example of the results of the failure to follow this rule. In 1960, Louisiana created a State Bond and Building Commission which was authorized to issue $60 million of revenue-type public improvement bonds, supported by a pledge of the General Fund revenues of the state; by this action the state government avoided submitting the issue to a vote of the people and authorized the new agency to expend the proceeds as well as issue the bonds. In the 1962 session of the Louisiana Legislature a second such agency, known as the Louisiana Fiscal Authority, was created to issue another $60 million of revenue-type bonds to be secured by 7 per cent of the sales tax revenues of the state. The first $20 million of the latter authorization sold on July 25, 1962, to a single syndicate bidder at interest rates on late maturities that extended up to 4.27 per cent. Louisiana is accustomed to paying higher rates than other states because of the state's complex debt structure and inefficient debt management procedures, but these exceed rates paid by Louisiana in the middle of the Depression when few other states were even attempting to borrow.

most appropriate method of financing. The capital improvement budget and the long-range financial plan for its support provide important evidence to the investor that a given state is doing a sound and responsible job of administering its financial affairs.[13]

The capital budget should include projects which produce self-generating income, such as toll bridges, port facilities, and college dormitories, as well as projects which must be financed from tax and other revenue sources. Project priorities, the methods of financing, and the types of borrowing to be utilized should be determined with care. A reappraisal of a state's debt issuing machinery is likely to be a valuable by-product of the adoption of the capital budgeting process. Capital improvement needs are also likely to be more adequately met and more efficiently financed.

General Obligation vs. Revenue Bonds

Revenue bond financing evolved from the "special fund doctrine." The courts held that capital expenditure projects of state governments which were entirely self-supporting did not involve the state's taxing power and thus were not subject to state constitutional debt limitations. This interpretation was later extended to include projects financed through the sale of obligations secured by specified and limited tax revenues but not supported by the full-faith-and-credit of the state. Both types of obligations came to be known as revenue bonds although the term originally referred to bonds serviced exclusively from the self-generated earnings of publicly owned facilities such as utilities. The first important use of these two types of obligations developed during the 1930's. By 1960, only about one half of the total long-term debt of state governments was in the form of general obligations. The other half, which is labeled "non-guaranteed debt" by the Bureau of Census, consisted of revenue-type bonds.[14]

There is little doubt that the main cause of this rapid adoption

---

[13] Smith, "Sound Financing for Sound Municipal Credit," 122.

[14] Bureau of the Census, *Compendium of State Government Finances in 1960*, 40; and Gottlieb, "The Revenue Bond and Public Debt," 31–32.

of the revenue or non-guaranteed type of obligation has been the existence of highly restrictive constitutional debt limitations in many of the states. A second important factor would appear to be the eagerness with which various groups in the bond market have accepted these obligations.

The financing of capital improvement projects through the dedication of specified tax or other revenues to support the issue of revenue-type bonds avoids state debt limitations, but there is a price attached to this privilege. First, investment bankers normally require more outside scrutiny and counsel, at the ultimate expense of the borrower, when revenue obligations are involved. There is also a greater tendency for issues to be negotiated rather than sold through competitive bidding.[15] It is not intended to imply here that such practices are not appropriate in many cases. Such actions do protect the bond holder but are also productive of fees. The latter fact partially explains the popularity of revenue bonds among investment bankers.

The other part of the price of the privilege of avoiding debt restrictions by issuing revenue-type bonds is the fact that these bonds usually involve higher interest costs than do full-faith-and-credit bonds. The cost differential will vary from issue to issue and from time to time but will generally range from .25 per cent to 1 per cent.[16] Roland Robinson, in his study of the postwar market for state and local bonds, simply concludes that "this penalty is often material." [17] Many observers have been surprised by the magnitude of the differential which has persisted in a period which has seen yield differentials between grades of corporate bonds narrow. A duplication of the worst loss experiences in the history of American municipals would be more than offset by the risk premium the market has required on most issues of revenue

[15] Almost a third of revenue obligations were negotiated in 1957 while only 4 per cent of full-faith-and-credit bond issues were marketed in this manner. Investment Bankers Association, *Statistical Bulletin*, XI, 8.

[16] Gottlieb, "The Revenue Bond and Public Debt," 38.

[17] Roland L. Robinson, *Postwar Market for State and Local Government Securities* (Princeton: Princeton University Press, 1960), 17.

bonds in the post-World War II period.[18] The fact that many state revenue bond issues are not rated by Moody's and Standard and Poor's while most general obligation issues do receive advance bond ratings may account in part for the interest cost disadvantage of unrated issues. However, traditional and established market patterns and conventional methods of appraising risk differentials would seem to account for the general magnitude of the penalty imposed by the market on revenue bond issues.

A final characteristic of revenue bond financing, which may involve added costs, is that the agencies which issue these bonds tend to be overspecialized. Specialization has its advantages, but it can be carried too far, and this is what happens when there are many agencies doing a state's borrowing. The lack of efficiency which tends to follow the use of numerous borrowing units has been aptly linked with the phenomenon of sub-optimization. Sub-optimization usually refers to the disadvantages that result when problems are parceled out for piecemeal analysis and solution.[19] With wise capital budgeting and financial planning, in the absence of constitutional debt limitations, one would certainly expect a state government to make little use of revenue bonds.

The characteristics of general obligation issues are well known and involve little uncertainty when debt management is efficient. Revenue bonds, on the other hand, frequently have complex histories and have such unique and untested characteristics that they are sometimes referred to as "story" bonds. General obligations are also superior to revenue obligations because they are secured by highly diversified revenue sources while revenue bonds are usually protected by a single source of funds. This narrow base makes the revenue bond much more vulnerable to unexpected difficulties.[20] Even in cases involving income-earning projects that

[18] John L. O'Donnell, "Some Postwar Trends in Municipal Bond Financing," *Journal of Finance*, XVII (May, 1962), 259–61, 264.

[19] Gottlieb, "The Revenue Bond and Public Debt," 41; and Roland N. McKean, *Efficiency in Government Through Systems Analysis* (New York: Wiley, 1958), 29–43.

[20] Daniel M. Kelly, "The Prospective Market for Municipal Securities," *Municipal Finance*, XXXI (August, 1958), 14–15; and Gottlieb, "The Revenue Bond and Public Debt," 41.

are expected to be self-supporting, full-faith-and-credit financing may be preferable. General obligations issued to finance such a project will be backed by both the self-generated income of the project and the full-faith-and-credit of the state; the results in all such cases should be lower costs of financing and a commensurate advantage for the users of the services of the facilities financed.

Over-all capital budgeting and financial planning for public improvements could be instituted without legal changes in most states. The results of such action would be substantial economies and great gains in administrative efficiency. The solution to the problem of excessive use of expensive revenue bond financing must await elimination or revision of constitutional debt limitations in many states. States with this problem should seek a relaxation of legal restraints on the use of general obligation bonds when bond financing of public improvements is appropriate.

Margin of Protection and Safety

Although debt to property tax assessment ratios are no longer usable measures of the margin of protection and safety in the case of state bond issues, some state constitutions still contain such references. Equally anachronistic market conventions are today still given some weight by investors, investment bankers, and the rating services. For example, an unlimited *ad valorem* tax pledge in a state's constitution may get favorable comment from one of the above mentioned groups, while the absence of such a pledge in a state which has abandoned the state *ad valorem* tax or has a constitutional limit on its *ad valorem* tax rate may get unfavorable mention. In similiar fashion, the bond market still looks with great favor on such legal semantics as "mandatory," "required," "judicially enforceable," "unlimited taxes," and "first charge" in bond indentures. Rigorous sinking fund arrangements are also sometimes required even when serial bonds are being issued.

Unlike the above, the following conventional market criteria of safety are not anachronistic, but some question may be raised relative to the weight assigned them and the need for greater use of other basic criteria. For example, in the case of full-faith-and-credit state bonds, great attention is given to ratios of specifically pledged revenues to debt service charges on specific issues and to the lien positions of successive issues. Where the ratios are not spelled out in the bond indenture, speculation arises as to whether the full-faith-and-credit pledge does in fact give the bond holder a first claim on other state revenues not required for the servicing of other bonded indebtedness. Much attention is given to provisions for subsequent issues. Where the practice of pledging specific revenues and giving subsidiary lien positions to successive issues is followed in the case of full-faith-and-credit bonds, market conventions tend to relegate such issues to a position little stronger than that of non-guaranteed bonds.[21]

Perhaps the most effective step that any state could take to strengthen the security provisions of its general obligations would be to establish a debt service fund that would supersede all other funds and through which all state tax and non-tax revenues (except perhaps intergovernmental receipts earmarked for certain purposes) would pass. In this way state bond holders could be given a clear and unequivocal first charge against the total revenues of the state, and this additional legal assurance could be given to bond holders without upsetting any of the existing allocations or dedications of revenues to specific operating functions.[22] The state would need only to make sure that sufficient funds were available in the bond fund to service outstanding debts; the rest of the revenues flowing through the fund would never be tapped. Only funds already pledged to the support of outstanding bond issues would not be channeled through this special bond fund, and provisions would be made for all future general obligation bonds of the state to be issued on a par basis. With this one step, a state could eliminate permanently the onus

[21] Failure to observe the requirements of conventional market standards and inadequate reporting have unquestionably cost the state of Louisiana millions of dollars in unnecessary interest charges since the beginning of the present structure of debt and debt management in this state which dates from the 1920's.

[22] Ross and Bonin, "A Proposed New System of Non-Highway Bond Financing for Louisiana," 367.

of subsidiary liens on its general obligations and the temptation to issue future revenue-type bonds supported by specific tax levies. At the same time, it would guarantee all future bond holders the maximum margin of protection and safety in terms of ratio of pledged revenues to debt service charges.

It is encouraging to note that this approach to debt security has recently been adopted in Puerto Rico and that debt service has priority on all available revenues in the Commonwealth.[23] This provision, together with the flexible debt limit referred to above, makes the constitution of Puerto Rico a model one insofar as debt management is concerned.[24]

Unfortunately, few state governments may be expected to follow this example in the near future. Without such action, however, there would appear to be full justification for a re-examination of conventional market criteria. The market and the rating services do give some attention to a state's economic base, its current wealth and economic development, its natural resources, and its potential for future economic development, but there are no well-established and widely accepted measures of these factors in use. Neither are there any established criteria for appraising the revenue base and the broad general fiscal powers of state governments.

In the case of state bonds, it would seem to be both economically sound and appropriate for the market and the rating services to give specific attention and greater weight to certain broad measures of the state's ability to meet its debt obligations. Direct use could be made of standards such as the ratio of borrowing to total state revenues, the ratio of borrowing to total state expenditures, the ratio of annual debt service payments to total state revenues, the ratio of borrowing to annual debt redemption payments, the ratio of annual interest charges to total state reve-

---

[23] "Municipal Finance Newsletter" (January 1, 1962), 2.

[24] A similar reorganization of highway debt management machinery only was effected in the state of Louisiana in 1955 with one of the co-authors of this paper, William D. Ross, acting as consultant to the Louisiana Department of Highways and the Joint House-Senate Highway Committee of the State Legislature. See Article 6, Section 23, Louisiana Constitution.

nues, and the ratio of annual debt redemption payments to total state debt.[25]

Questions raised about the validity of bond ratings and of conventional market criteria do not, of course, absolve the states from making certain that they are not victims of the conventional standards. Bond ratings are important because they are used by investors as an indication of credit standings and because they bear a clear relationship to interest charges that must be paid for borrowed funds. Other things being equal, the higher the rating, the lower the interest cost. Thus, if the factors affecting ratings are known, the method of lowering interest costs should be very clear. Careful consideration of conventional market rules which influence ratings and interest costs is still of great importance. It is here maintained only that some new and perhaps more appropriate standards may be needed for the proper appraisal of state bonds. Revised emphasis may also need to be given to some existing standards which are still applicable.

Surely, when it is apparent that a state's economy is strong and that it has every intention of honoring its obligations, a penalty of as much as 1 per cent because of a cluttered state debt structure is heavy indeed. Current market standards as reflected in state bond ratings are not ultimate criteria. All factors considered, it would seem logical to expect that the bonds of a state would usually receive equal or higher ratings and enjoy lower interest costs than the bonds of its political subdivisions. Such is not the case in some states. This is certainly not a plea for lower ratings for local bonds. Rather, it is a case for more thorough and more realistic appraisals of state bonds by the rating services and the market. Perhaps separate systems of symbols for rating state and local bonds would also be helpful.

Reporting

Inadequate reporting appears to be an almost inevitable result

---

[25] It is obvious that this approach is less applicable and would be difficult to apply to local bond issues.

of the fractionating of a state's debt management responsibilities. Everybody's business is nobody's business under these circumstances. Information can be supplied to the market and the rating services on specific issues, but no one assumes responsibility for supplying the information that would give a complete picture of the total state debt structure and the interrelationships of its parts.

In discussing the importance of reporting, Wade S. Smith states:

> Soundly contrived plans and well arranged debt structure will avail the community but little if the investor is not informed about them. . . . Few investors, however, are equipped to collect at first hand all the information they require, and if they were, public officials would be deluged with more inquires than they could conceivably handle. In practice, the information gap is closed by the independent credit reporting agency, which collects, analyzes, and publishes the information pertinent to an appraisal of the credit quality of the bonds. . . .
>
> Nonetheless, no appraisal of the bonds of any municipality is feasible unless certain essential information is provided by the municipality itself.[26]

The types of information normally communicated in debt reporting have been categorized as follows: (1) historical information, (2) current and capital budget information, and (3) details about new bond issues. The historical information is of interest to rating agencies, investment bankers, and investors. Current and capital budget information will interest all of these groups plus taxpayers and is of special interest to prospective bidders when new issues are advertised. Among the details that should be reported in advertisements for bids are the purpose of the issue, the security of the bonds, and the authorized but unissued obligations.[27]

Perhaps there should be still another category of debt report-

[26] Smith, "Sound Financing for Sound Municipal Credit," 124–25.
[27] *Ibid.*

ing to supply information to holders of outstanding obligations. This type of reporting might have a salutary influence on future bond sales through its effect on the price of outstanding obligations. Proper reporting of improvements in the economic base or in political or legal institutions can cause the price of outstanding issues to increase, and the good will that this appreciation can cause among current bond holders would tend to create a better market for later issues.[28]

Bond Contract Provisions

As noted earlier in this paper, operational procedures concerning such matters as the denomination of bonds, type of bonds (serial or term), sinking fund provisions, maturities, call feature, and timing should be left to the discretion of the borrowing agency. Such freedom is necessary in order for that agency to cope with changing conditions in the bond market.

For example, larger bond denominations apparently are gaining popularity among investors.[29] Since there is presently no disadvantage to a state's credit in issuing these large denominations, there should be no hesitation in providing them when it appears that they are in demand, if there are no legal restrictions on size of denominations within a given state.

With respect to type of bond and maturities, some well-established principles may be noted. In general, bonds should begin to mature reasonably promptly where a capital project is involved; maturities should not extend beyond the probable life of the project being financed; and level or declining annual debt service payments are preferable. Straight serial bonds involve equal annual principal payments and result in declining annual charges for principal and interest combined, thus affording greatest financial flexibility for the issuing government. Serial-annuity type bonds require level annual debt service payments since

[28] George T. Ragsdale, "Revenue Bond Financing and Interest Rate Trends," *Commercial and Financial Chronicle*, CLXXXVI (July 4, 1957), 3.

[29] Felix T. Davis, "Bond Denominations—$5,000 Units Now and Commonplace," *The Daily Bond Buyer*, Municipal Finance Officers Association, Special Conference Issue No. 1 (May 2, 1962), 25.

principal maturities rise as interest charges decline. The latter type of issue is appropriate in cases of very large projects or self-liquidating projects where earning capacity is expected to develop slowly.

Deferred serials, which make no retirement of principal for a period of time, and irregular serials, which may have any pattern of maturities, are not desirable types of debt instruments except in rare cases where they can be used to correct a pre-existing weakness in the debt structure of a state or local government. Term bonds have been almost completely replaced by the use of serial issues. The latter avoid the difficulties associated with sinking funds and are also preferable to the lender because they make easier the acquisition of bonds maturing at times which are peculiarly suited to needs of the individual investor.[30]

The call option should be reserved when it is not too expensive to do so, but determining whether it is appropriate is mostly a matter of judgment and will depend upon circumstances in the borrowing state as well as general market conditions.[31] This problem should be left in the hands of the borrowing authority together with that of deciding if and when to call bonds, if the option has been reserved.

The final operational procedures to be discussed here are the issue procedure and the timing of sales. Under normal circumstances, competitive bidding is always preferable to negotiated sales of state bonds. The issue procedure entails advertising for bids. It has been noted above that the official invitation or advertisement for bids should be accompanied by complete reporting of all information pertinent to a new issue. The time schedule on which this information is made available can be highly important since the market for the bonds becomes greater as the story of the issue becomes more widely known. Again quoting Wade Smith:

[30] Smith, "Sound Financing for Sound Municipal Credit," 124; David M. Ellinwood, "Guideposts to Success in Debt Management," Municipal Finance, XXIX (February, 1957), 115–16.

[31] The call feature is discussed at length by E. Lynn Crossley, "Value of Call Feature in Municipal Bonds," *Municipal Finance*, XXX (August, 1957), *passim.*

Some of the larger states and communities, with established markets for their bonds, can sometimes sell successfully on fairly short notice, but the prospective borrower who is in the market infrequently is always well advised to give ample notice and have all official statements available promptly. If plenty of advance notice is given, if planned financing is soundly conceived and executed, and if adequate information is provided explaining the program and giving all relevant data about the community's (state's) finances, the finance officer can be satisfied that he has done everything possible to assure that the bonds will be sold on the best terms then available.[32]

One dimension of the timing factor is worthy of note. Bert Betts, state treasurer of California, has recently instituted a policy of offering bonds in smaller amounts and only when market conditions are considered favorable. This approach is unorthodox and has been criticized in the market, but it would appear to have considerable merit. Thus far, it seems to have accomplished its objectives of garnering more bids on state issues and allowing the state to take advantage of the opportunity to sell its bonds when market conditions appear to be favorable.[33]

Data presented in Table 4 indicate that there may be a significant seasonal pattern which could be important in timing state (and local) borrowing. Since state (and local) units are subject to little pressure as to the exact moment of availability of public improvements and if yields are relatively and significantly lower at certain times of the year (on the average), then the state could profit in the long run by floating its issues during the months that are generally more favorable. If significant amounts of state and local borrowing were timed to take advantage of this seasonal pattern, of course, this action would tend to level the seasonal fluctuation.

[32] Smith, "Sound Financing for Sound Municipal Credit," 125.
[33] Bert A. Betts, "How to Approach Planning for Present and Future Needs," *The Daily Bond Buyer*, Municipal Finance Officers Association, Special Conference Issue No. 2 (June 11, 1962). See also "Wall Street Talks," *Business Week* (June 17, 1961), 142; "In the Markets," *Business Week* (August 26, 1961), 73.

Future Needs

Obviously, the need for public improvements in this country will continue to expand as our population increases, the urbanization process accelerates, and our way of life grows more complex.[34]

TABLE 4

SEASONAL INDEX OF YIELDS OF STATE AND
LOCAL BONDS RATED BAA*

Month	Percent of normal Based on the mean	Based on the median
January	99.8	99.7
February	97.8	98.2
March	97.5	97.7
April	97.2	95.4
May	97.4	98.4
June	97.8	97.3
July	98.5	98.9
August	101.9	102.1
September	104.0	105.2
October	101.7	101.0
November	103.4	105.6
December	102.3	100.6

Source: Computed from information available in the *Federal Reserve Bulletin*, 1955–58, Vol. 41–44, and April, 1959.

* This index was constructed by centering 12-month moving averages. The monthly yields used in this computation date from November, 1954, to March, 1959, inclusive. Joseph M. Bonin, "A Critical Analysis of the Debt Structure and Debt Management in Louisiana" (Ph.D. dissertation, Louisiana State University, 1960).

There will be great pressure, therefore, for more state borrowing both in states which have borrowed heavily in the past and in states which heretofore have done little borrowing. In most states poor planning and execution of debt financing do exist. Gottlieb has focused on the increasing use of revenue bonds as the main

[34] Otto Eckstein, *Trends in Public Expenditures in the Next Decade* (a supplementary paper of the Committee for Economic Development, April, 1959), 5–10.

symptom of the "growing obsolescence and disjuncture in our public economy." [35] O'Donnell notes especially the problem of overlapping jurisdictions and muses that "it will be fascinating to see how our traditional inventiveness meets the tremendous challenge of providing for the public sector of the economy." [36]

It is our recommendation that state governments begin by getting their own debt houses in order and then that they give consideration to means by which they may be able to assist their political subdivisions. State guarantees of local bonds and state coordination of local debt financing may prove to be feasible means of giving such assistance. If the states do not take such action to assist the municipalities and other local units of government, the federal government may eventually be expected to do so. The new schools, colleges, highways, streets, hospitals, and other public facilities are needed not in Washington, D.C., but at the state and local levels. It will require the combined ingenuity and cooperation of state and local finance officers, investment bankers, bond attorneys, financial service agencies, economists, and politicians to find solutions to the challenge we confront in this area. When and if solutions are found, public understanding will be essential to their adoption.

These solutions will not be aided by uncritical allegiance to existing conventions observed by borrowers and lenders in the bond market today. In particular, it would appear that the states should return to the extensive use of simpler and sounder general obligation borrowing for their long-term capital needs. Rating services, in turn, should recognize the extremely high quality of most state obligations and should revitalize their rating systems. The rating agencies and investors should realize that while they may be able to discern some differences in the risks between various state obligations, the magnitude of the differential needs to be re-examined. The exaggeration of these differentials will only make it more difficult, if not impossible, for future capi-

[35] Gottlieb, "The Revenue Bond and Public Debt," 42.
[36] O'Donnell, "Some Postwar Trends in Municipal Bond Financing, " 268.

tal improvement needs to be met at the state and local levels. It is our contention that the risk of permanent default on any state's bonds today is not materially greater than that for U.S. Treasury obligations.

NEW DIMENSIONS OF THE CAPITALIZATION OF EARNINGS IN APPRAISING PUBLIC UTILITY PROPERTY

James W. Martin

THE APPRAISAL PEOPLE—whether researchers, practitioners, or courts—agree that, though many kinds of adaptations are essential to sound practice, there are three basic ways in which a valuation task involving a complex property can be tackled.[1] Each has its place in the estimation of the price at which property would most likely be sold in a competitive market where would-be sellers and would-be buyers are free from compulsion.[2] An enumeration of these three methods with a very brief sketch of each will prove helpful.

Under certain conditions the so-called summation approach is relevant and fruitful. Generally, this attack applies to a complex situation if whole units of the complex property are being currently reproduced *and* if new units are similar in character and are in direct competition with the existing holdings to be valued. Otherwise this method is not relevant. Under usual market conditions a wide range of complex properties meets these requirements, for instance, homes and small retail and service buildings. Summation based on some conception or variant of cost is an important appraisal tool; and indeed, it is the only tool frequently used in tax appraisals because we have to resort to what has come to be called mass appraisals. That is, we have to do it at very low cost per unit.

The second method is referred to as the comparison method or sometimes comparative sales analysis. This approach to finding the value of bare land is so usual and so convincing that, in situ-

---

[1] The point is examined and documented in James W. Martin and Milford Estill, *Valuation of Property: Economic and Legal Standards* (Lexington: Bureau of Business Research, 1949, and *Kentucky Law Journal*, November, 1949), 7–30.

[2] This seems to be the practical, statistical formulation of the lawyer's willing-buyer-willing-seller conception.

148

ations in which low-cost appraisal is necessary, it frequently crowds out all other approaches. But comparison is a valuation tool that is useful in a considerable number and variety of other situations, some of them characterized by greater complexity than bare land.

The third approach involves the estimation of property values by the capitalization of earnings method. That is to say, the earnings produced by the property are capitalized to produce an estimate of the value. In most appraisals of operating businesses or other productive plants, this method is quite commonly utilized, and it produces rather accurate results in the case of properties that are not unique. For business use in evaluating more complex property than bare land or usual dwellings, capitalization of earnings probably has a broader range of applications than either of the other two approaches. However, it is important to keep in mind that capitalization can be grossly abused.

Each of these three ways of tackling a valuation problem seems at first observation to precipitate more difficulties than it resolves. At the same time a good appraiser must employ all three attacks to the extent that they are economically available and relevant to the particular valuation problem.[3]

Appraisal of Public Service Properties

In the valuation for tax and numerous other purposes, the size of the railroad or other public utility operating unit[4] is often such that the state can well afford to spend enough to do a thoroughly

[3] Generally, "economically available" means merely that for the particular appraisal enough money is available to make possible the use of the approach. For example, for purposes of tax assessment of small business and residence properties, "mass appraisals" are often made. This in a particular case may mean using only comparison as to land values and only estimated cost of replacement (or reproduction) less allowances for depreciation, including obsolescence of buildings. Compare Martin and Estill, *Valuation of Property*, 7–30.

[4] The unit to be valued, often interstate in character, is the operating entity. For example, one corporation may own a whole property in this sense; but, especially in the case of railroads, much of the property may be leased or controlled through stock ownership. The latter means are especially usual in the case of electric and of gas and electric concerns.

good appraisal job even at considerable aggregate cost. Since the appraisal cost per unit of value is low, a large aggregate expenditure for appraisal may be justified in these cases. And, in some applications, all of the basic methods can and, in the interest of good practice, must be used. For example, a new public service plant is usually best appraised by cost summation if it has been constructed as one project or as a group of projects. As the plant is operated it may prove to be either more or less profitable than originally anticipated. Thus, as operating experience is accumulated, cost becomes irrelevant, and other attacks which take account of the operating experience become exclusively persuasive.

Since the remainder of this paper is devoted in the main to the capitalization of earnings method, it may be helpful to explain parenthetically that the comparison method applied to public service corporation properties, whether railroad, air line, water works, electric power, or what have you, is handled in a somewhat unusual fashion. Because whole operating entities are rarely sold in the open market, one must usually find another kind of comparison or abandon the method. It is customary and often meaningful to find the selling prices of stocks, bonds or other long-term loans, and current and deferred liabilities, and to assume that their total or aggregate value is equal to all the property of the company or companies, that is, to the total assets if the enterprise is solvent. This merely means that assets are equal to liabilities if the proprietorship of the corporation or corporate group is included among the liabilities. For example, electric power companies are frequently operated by a holding company employing a number of subsidiary corporations. In this case the valuation unit is the corporate group rather than the individual corporation. This stock and debt method is a valuable appraisal tool when all the securities are on the open market. The stock and debt method can be used with less precision when the stock is regularly bought and sold but when other security prices must be estimated by comparison with the obligations of similar corporations. However, the use of the particular tool is rapidly diminishing by reason of changes in the financing policies of public utility corporations.

Capitalization of Earnings

An increasing number of the public utility corporations are selling their securities in private markets so that security quotations from the New York Stock Exchange or some other organized market are not available.

The capitalization of the earnings produced by the property of a corporation or corporate group engaged in the public service has long been a valid and rather precise method of appraising corporate property.[5] It is now widely recognized[6] that there are two fundamental problems of major importance in using this approach. (1) What is the appropriate definition of the measure of earnings to be employed? (2) At what rate shall the earnings as defined be capitalized?

Historically speaking, each of these queries was answered irrationally and, if refined appraisal is to be considered the objective, very unfortunately for about sixty years following the U.S. Supreme Court's decision in 1875 in State Railroad Tax Cases,[7] in which this unit method of valuation was emphatically recognized. From the time that uniform public utility accounts were set up,

[5] In addition to the documentation previously cited, it may be helpful to refer to Roswell C. McCrea, "The Taxation of Transportation Companies in the United States," *Report* of *the United States Industrial Commission*, 1901, IX; James C. Bonbright, *The Valuation of Property* (New York: McGraw-Hill, 1937); Board of Investigation and Research, *Carrier Taxation* (Washington, D.C.: Government Printing Office, 1944); James W. Martin, *Research Report to the Virginia Public Service Tax Study Committee* (Richmond, Va.: The Committee, 1947), and *Valuation of Arizona Rail, Telephone, and Telegraph Properties* (Phoenix: Division of Appraisal and Assessment Standards, 1965). The bulk of the new material reported in this paper is drawn from a series of unpublished reports the writer prepared for Commissioner J. E. Luckett, Kentucky Department of Revenue, 1966 and 1967. It is used with Mr. Luckett's permission.

It is perhaps superfluous to indicate that the earnings concerned are those in prospect for the normally well-managed enterprise. If a business is such a normally well-managed undertaking, historical data may be decidedly useful.

[6] Committee on Unit Valuation, *Appraisal of Railroad and Other Public Utility Property for Ad Valorem Tax Purposes* (Chicago: National Association of Tax Administrators, 1954), Chapters 7 and 8; James W. Martin, "Assessment of Public Utility Property" (a report prepared for the Kentucky Department of Revenue, 1954), 31–50, and the materials there cited; and Martin, *Valuation of Arizona Rail, Telephone, and Telegraph Properties*. Frederick L. Bird and Edna T. Bird, *Role of the States in Strengthening the Property Tax* (Washington, D.C.: Advisory Commission on Intergovernmental Relations, 1963), I, 156–61, take account of the basic issues.

[7] 92 U.S. 575 (1875).

it was assumed that the income after all taxes (including income taxes) had been deducted was the appropriate earnings measure for capitalization. This assumption was not fully discredited,[8] and the intellectual void was not even partly filled, until the early 1950's.

The assumptions regarding the appropriate rate or rates of capitalization were equally misguided. The appropriate rate was sometimes assumed to be the "legal" rate for loans! It was overlooked that various securities were sold on a national market at various rates of return while the legal rate was fixed by law in each state and varied from one to the other. Although this was common knowledge, the two rates were never reconciled. Some tried to identify the appropriate rate with that fixed in connection with determining the regulatory rate base. Other persons had still other irrelevant criteria.

The National Association of Tax Administrators' report and the Kentucky study,[9] both written in 1954 and to a very considerable extent conducted independently of one another, attempted to find a market relationship between capital value, the appraisal sought, and the more objective measures of earnings. In the Kentucky study it was established that various measures of earnings could be properly employed; the study demonstrated that operating revenue, that is, gross receipts from the utility business, in certain applications was a better measure than income in accord with any of the standard definitions.[10] This possibility had been suggested at one time by as eminent a scholar as Thomas S. Adams—at that time with the University of Wisconsin and later with Yale University until his death. Adams is often referred

---

[8] Compare James W. Martin, "Corporate Taxes and the Assessment of Operating Property," *Journal of Land and Public Utility Economics* (August, 1940), 262 ff.

[9] Committee on Unit Valuation, *Appraisal of Railroad and Other Public Utility Property for Ad Valorem Tax Purposes*, and Martin, "Assessment of Public Utility Property."

[10] As shown in James W. Martin, "Obsolescence and the Assessment of Public Service Properties," *Proceedings . . . National Tax Association*, 1960, 410 ff., the superiority of operating revenue as the best of the three measures tested continued through 1957.

to as the father of the United States income tax law. That is a slight exaggeration, but he had a tremendous influence on the development of the federal income tax.

As the Kentucky study of the early 1950's and that of the railroads in the late 1950's involved in part an objective determination of capitalization rates and a statistical measure of the reliability of each rate distinctly similar to the method followed in a more recent Kentucky investigation, it is of interest to undertake a comparson of the results.[11] As a preliminary to this kind of analysis a very brief, nontechnical summary of the method of estimating rates of capitalization on the basis of historical data is appropriate.

In general, to find the rate at which the market capitalizes a particular earnings measure, we divide the measure chosen by the known capital value. This, of course, is an extremely simple and well known financial generalization. In the attempt to apply it, that is, in finding the rate at which the evidence of receipts or of income is capitalized, one encounters two major difficulties: (1) how to ascertain the capital value, that is, how may the value of the property actually become "known"; and (2) how to deal with the fact that many public service corporations, notably railroad companies, own both property employed in the utility business as well as other property. Among the major systems that I have had occasion to appraise in connection with regular consulting assignments are the Santa Fe and the Southern Pacific railroads. Both of these carriers now have more nonoperating property than railroad property. In the case of the Southern Pacific, this is only partly true, or at least its absolute truth is unconfirmed, because the Southern Pacific Company figures were used instead of consolidated figures. The Santa Fe figures were

---

[11] As set out in a June 10, 1966, memorandum to Commissioner Luckett of the Kentucky Department of Revenue, there are differences in the methods used in the various studies. The refinements, however, seem not to invalidate the comparisons. The variations, on the contrary, are probably due to developments in (a) utility corporate size, structure, and operations; (b) the securities market; (c) public regulation; (d) taxation, especially at the federal level; and (e) other operating or environmental factors affecting public service corporation experience.

consolidated so that all the railroad property owned by Santa Fe and its associates was included within the unit.

Method of Study

All students who have tackled the first problem, that is, the determination of capital value, seem to have accepted stock and debt valuations of corporations for which good quotations were available as the basic method of estimating the full value of corporate property.[12] Certainly, this is the primary approach of the Kentucky studies. In both of these statistical approaches of the early 1950's and of the mid-1960's, attempts to gather information as to whole public service corporation sales were only partially successful. The number of sales located was limited, and the facts regarding many of them were incomplete. However, the meager sales data assembled,[13] about thirty cases of all kinds of public service corporations, seemed roughly to conform with stock and debt values. The procedure was to compute the rates of capitalization using both measures and compare the rates derived. It does not happen in any one of these thirty odd cases that the same corporation for which stock and debt values were available was also the corporation that was sold, so the test had to be an indirect test. In other words, the rates of capitalization were tested rather than the value as such. But since it is necessary to use the value as fixed by the two methods, it amounts to the same thing or substantially the same thing.

The second query, relating to the public utility corporation ownership of both property used in the public service and property not so employed, is answered in terms of a large number of

[12] There are technical objections; there are many more reasons for the discard of available alternatives.

The stock and debt estimates of value properly made are usually deemed to be reasonably precise on an industry basis even though subject to considerable error on the basis of a particular corporation or corporate group. That historical data are employed is rarely deemed to introduce serious error.

[13] In the study of data for 1964, about thirty such sales of various utility properties as wholes were found; but some of the facts were so incomplete as to be useless; some, partly useful; and a few, very convincing as far as one case can convince.

rather technical adjustments, especially where corporate groups, often parent and subsidiary corporations, are involved. The problem is handled by combining receipts or income, as the case may be, from both kinds of property and so, in effect, assuming that the two sorts of property produce the same rate of earnings. This procedure introduces some error in the estimates; but, aside from railroad corporations, the property owners' nonoperating property is almost invariably a statistically small matter. There is some evidence that, even in the instance of rail carriers, the error from this maneuver is not of great magnitude.

Four measures of earnings have attracted so much attention that they are examined in the recent Kentucky study: (a) operating revenue, that is, the gross receipts from the conduct of the public service business, (b) net operating income before the deduction of any taxes or depreciation,[14] (c) net operating income after all depreciation and business taxes but before the deduction of taxes measured by income, and (d) net operating income after the deduction of all taxes and depreciation. As a result of two comprehensive Kentucky canvasses of all these possibilities (except the second, which was studied only in the recent Kentucky undertaking in 1964), the conclusion seems clear that an appraiser should employ two, three, or four of these rates[15] in practice and should average the estimates derived from each. Two or three measures can usually be established as definitely superior, and other possibilities simply can be ignored.

The next question relates to the method of distinguishing the superior from the mediocre measure of earnings from the viewpoint of estimating capital value, *i.e.*, the most probable selling

---

[14] Dr. Ronald B. Welch, "Refinements in the Capitalization-of-Earnings Approach to Valuation of Public Utility Properties," *Proceedings . . . National Tax Association*, 1955, 99 ff., shows reason for thinking this rate, if properly established, is sounder as an appraisal tool than are those relating to other measures of earnings. See also p. 119 of the same volume.

[15] There are occasional cases in which one method is so clearly superior that only it is used. The text is formulated deliberately to ignore this exceptional possibility, which may exist only in relation to R.E.A. borrowers.

price if the property were sold.[16] This problem was first worked out in the earlier of the two major Kentucky studies[17] and can be resolved in terms of the deviation of the rates for individual corporations or corporate groups from the average for all taxpayers studied. In the early 1950's a coefficient of variation was computed by dividing the standard deviation by the mean. For technical reasons this seemed superior to the use of standard error as a method of dealing with the situation. In the 1964 study this method and also a coefficient of dispersion computed from the means were examined. In both cases the capitalization rates were weighted by a commonsense inference from the dispersion measures themselves. In other words, after developing an estimate of values by means of each of these measures, the results are weighted in keeping with the showing in the dispersion figures. If the dispersion is low then the estimate deserves a higher rating than if the dispersion is high. Thus, a system of weighting which emphasizes the good capitalization rates and de-emphasizes the relatively poor ones may be designed. In all cases observed it has been possible to have general acceptance of the weights once the dispersion measures had been determined.

The data from which computations were made included figures for all of the corporations, as reported in Moody's manual, of each class for which satisfactory and relevant security quotations were available. The American, and in a few cases Canadian, taxpayers included seemed reasonably representative of all companies Moody reports except as to method of financing. It is not possible to be certain that the standards of relevance were identical in the study of the 1950's and in that of the mid-1960's. The general number and size characteristic of the corporations of each class actually included in the computations are shown in Table 5, which gives a considerable amount of information with

---

[16] Since the revenue or income data employed are "operating" figures, the value estimate by capitalization relates exclusively to property employed in operation, *i.e.*, in the provision of public service.

[17] James W. Martin, "New Evidence on Tax Valuation of Public Service Property—Capitalization of Earnings," *National Tax Journal* (December, 1954), 309 ff.

respect to the 1964 study and the number of corporations with respect to the earlier one.[18]

Comparisons of the results of the two general studies to the extent that coverage was the same[19] should answer numerous

TABLE 5

DATA ON WHICH NEW CAPITALIZATION
RATE COMPUTATIONS ARE BASED

Kind of Property	Actual Number of Corporations 1964	Actual Number of Corporations 1951–52	Theoretical Number* of Corporations	Taxpayers' Aggregate Revenue in Millions
Airline Co. Property	11	12	603	$2,729
Bus Co. Property—				
Urban Use	8	11	53	53
Electric Power Co.				
Property	39	39	833	5,771
Gas Distribution Co.				
Property	22	37	314	957
Electric and Gas				
Property	42	38	585	6,594
Motor Truck Co.				
Property—General	25	7	101	727
Railroad Property	33	49	3,746	5,438
Telephone Co. Property	15	30	6,483	2,953
Water Co. Property	10	21	73	48

*The "theoretical number" is computed by adding the weightings of the several corporations. The weight for each company is computed by dividing the operating revenue of the smallest into that of each particular corporation.

[18] Except for refinements and adaptations reported in the June 10, 1966, memorandum to Commissioner Luckett, the method and its history are explained more fully in note 6. Martin, "Obsolescence and the Assessment of Public Service Properties," 413; James W. Martin, "Marshalling the Evidence of the Value of Public Utility Property," *Proceedings . . . National Tax Association*, 1955, 110 ff. and the works cited on p. 110 of that paper.

[19] Some classes of companies are excluded from the comparison on the ground that the number of corporations was so limited that the results, though usable in default of anything better, have no research significance. These include barge lines, interurban buses, ferries, special classes of trucks other than those in general service, toll bridges, and the like. Gas transmission pipelines are omitted because in the 1954–55 reports a petroleum pipeline company was included among the gas transmission companies, and the gas and petroleum companies were separately examined as of 1964.

TABLE 6

CAPITALIZATION RATES, 1964 COMPARED WITH 1951–52

Rates

	I Operating Revenue		II Net Income before Income Tax		III Net Income after Income Tax	
	'64	'51–52	'64	'51–52	'64	'51–52
Airline Co. Property*	68%	116%	8.7%	12.3%	5.5%	6.2%
Bus Co. Property—Urban Use	110	158	7.9	11.0	5.0	6.6
Electric Power Co. Property	17	23	6.5	7.1	4.1	4.7
Electric and Gas Co. Property	22	27	6.3	7.4	4.3	4.7
Gas Distribution Co. Property	34	33	6.1	8.3	3.9	5.3
Motor Truck Co. Property	152	181	11.0	20.1	6.2	10.0
Railroad Co. Property	42	62	6.2	11.2	5.7	6.7
Telephone Co. Property	27	31	7.7	7.5	4.4	4.8
Water Co. Property	15	19	6.2	7.3	4.4	5.4

*The data for airlines were computed in the same general manner as were the other class of utilities for 1964, but in the early 1950's the nonoperating property was deducted af the corporate full values were estimated.

questions, among them the following. To what extent are the levels of capitalization rates identical or nearly so in 1951, 1952, and 1964? (In the early study all of the data were for 1951 except for railroads and the data there were for 1952, so we speak of that as the 1951–52 study.) Is the reliability of each capitalization rate greater, about the same, or reduced, as compared with results in the early 1950's? On the basis of the relative reliability of each of the several rates computed, what is the comparative appraisal importance of the several measures of earnings as a basis for value estimation by capitalization? These queries may well be considered in order.

Table 6 shows that every operating revenue capitalization rate used is sharply lower in 1964 than for 1951–52. Except in the case of telephone companies and capitalization of operating income before deduction of state, local, and federal income taxes, the same observation applies to rates of income capitalization. Similarly, all rates of capitalization of operating income after deducting all taxes, that is, the rates for every class of company reported

TABLE 6 *(cont.)*

Reliability

I				II				III			
δ/mean		Weight		δ/mean		Weight		δ/mean		Weight	
'64	'51–52	'64	'51–52	'64	'51–52	'64	'51–52	'64	'51–52	'64	'51–52
;.2%	22.4%	1	5	27.0%	48.0%	0	1	16.5%	38.5%	1	2
5.9	37.9	0	1	30.1	27.4	1	2	34.6	21.1	0	4
3.3	25.3	0	1	10.5	17.0	3	3	10.1	15.6	3	4
3.5	30.7	0	4	15.8	38.5	0	2	8.0	33.2	3	3
3.8	39.5	0	1	20.4	37.1	4	1	20.9	28.1	4	3
;.0	30.5	1	2	25.0	26.7	1	3	24.4	26.6	1	3
).1	30.0	1	3	23.7	34.6	2	2	17.8	28.1	3	3
".7	33.2	2	5	6.5	34.6	3	4	5.1	40.7	4	2
5.2	32.6	0	2	11.9	21.6	1	5	5.3	29.9	2	3

in Table 6, based on income after income taxes, are clearly below the corresponding rates of the early 1950's. There was an interim Kentucky study of railroad capitalization for 1957,[20] which showed the rates for capitalization of operating revenue and for income before income tax down fractionally from those rates of the early 1950's and the rate for capitalization of income after all taxes a little higher. On the whole, however, the rate-level situation in the late 1950's in view of the 1964 rates was surprisingly like that for the early 1950's.

The reliability of the capitalization rates is depicted by coefficients which measure dispersion and which are shown in the later columns of Table 6. The data disclose that, with the exception of intraurban bus company properties, the capitalization rates in 1964 were definitely more reliable than those in 1951–52. The extraordinarily low coefficients of dispersion in the case of telephone property as of 1964 suggest that the rates of capitalization

[20] Martin, "Obsolescence and the Assessment of Public Service Properties," 413–18.

must be phenomenally reliable in regard to such property. This is the case regardless of the measure of earnings involved. The urban bus company exception is inferentially due to the recent depression in that business, but data have not been marshaled to develop that or other explanations. The railroad capitalization rates for 1957 were less reliable than those for the early 1950's and much less reliable than those for 1964.

The most intriguing differences apparent from Table 6 may well be deemed to be the fluctuations in the weightings derived from the comparative measures of dispersion. In examining these the curious person will wish to keep in mind (a) that a fourth rate of capitalization, that for operating income before any tax or depreciation deductions, was computed in 1964 and, if relatively reliable, was used in the actual valuation procedures; and (b) that the coefficient of variation shown in Table 6 was computed and permitted to influence the weightings which are depicted in the table. This mean deviation from the mean coefficient is not shown in the table because it is not relevant in the comparisons. In the case of airlines, the weights in the mid-1960's for capitalization of revenue, of income before income taxes, and of income after all taxes were respectively one, zero, and one. The same values for the early 1950's showed weightings respectively of five, one, and two. (Income from operations before any taxes or depreciation was also weighted one in the recent study.) For the same respective earnings measures, the weights for power companies in 1964 were zero, three, and three, whereas a dozen years earlier the computations produced weights inferred to be one, three, and four. A more remarkable case is that of gas and electric companies which should be treated separately from straight power companies. For the gas and electric companies, the respective weights were zero, zero, three for the current study, and four, two, and three for that of the early 1950's. With respect to telephone company property,[21] the weightings determined from dispersion measurement for the rates

[21] Because of arguments that Bell companies which are partly owned by American Telephone and Telegraphy Company are different, tests were run only to find out that they were in 1964 substantially identical with so-called independent concerns.

for operating revenue, operating income before income taxes, and operating income after income taxes in the mid-1960's compared with those in the early 1950's were respectively two, three, and four and five, four, and two-one steps up, the other steps down. In short, the situation as to the relative valuation significance of these three capitalizations for telephone company property was exactly the reverse during the dozen-year interval.

These examples—along with others, which the curious individual may readily read from the table—suggest emphatically the conclusion that the relative valuation significance of different measures of earnings in the early 1950's had no necessary relationship to those in the mid-1960's. The evidence seems equally convincing that the notion that any one measure of earnings may be adopted and properly used over a long period is a figment of a lazy imagination and, in fact, is emphatically and obviously false. The examples also seem strongly to suggest, if they do not fully demonstrate, that two, three, or four measures of earnings, if properly capitalized and weighted, can yield a more defensible appraisal of public service property than can the capitalization of any single measure of earnings. Finally, in this particular connection, these data, when read in conjunction with other evidence produced in the Kentucky study but not all reported in the present paper, emphatically support one other conclusion: operating revenue, operating income before deducting any taxes or depreciation, operating income before income taxes, and operating income after all taxes are *all* valuable bases of earnings capitalization. Indeed, the 1964 Kentucky study shows clearly that for some class or classes of public service property valuation every one of the four capitalization techniques tested (each involving varying definitions of earnings) is the most useful in one or another setting.

In addition to the general check on the validity of capitalization rates based on different measures of earnings, there are supplementary elements which might be mentioned. The possibility that corporate or corporate group size may make a difference in the rate of capitalization can be handled very simply if the sample of taxpayers is of reasonable size and variety (note that some barely qualify under this criterion).[22] The corporations can be arrayed by size and capitalization rates for each half of those in each class computed. Such analysis discloses seemingly significant differences in the instance of almost all categories in the early 1950's and in the case of extremely few classes in the study of the mid-1960's. Indeed, as to the latter investigation only airlines and gas distribution companies appear to disclose meaningful differences between the rates for the large and for the smaller companies.

The second and third tests, though they may require diverse handling,[23] are reasonably conducted in this same context. The first of these is based on the hypothesis that over- or under-use of stock in a public utility's capitalization structure may influence the market reaction and, hence, the capitalization rates of the enterprise. This hypothesis can be tested, and was checked in both the Kentucky studies, by arraying the taxpayers on the basis of the percentage of the capital provided by common stock (all, of course, on a market basis). This test indicates that this factor was statistically significant in almost all classes of public service corporations in the early 1950's and very rarely so in the mid-1960's.

The final test had to do with the extent to which taxpayer net earnings available for fixed charges, or for dividends, were distributed. This test was accomplished by arraying corporations according to the proportion of income available for fixed charges paid out as rentals,[24] interest, and dividends.[25] The separate com-

---

[22] It will be kept in view that the methodology outlined in this paper is directly applicable only to earning corporations of the sizes reported in Moody's Manuals.

[23] See James W. Martin, "Valuing Utilities via Stock and Debt Estimates," *Public Utilities Fortnightly* (August 4, 1955), 161 ff. For another view as to dividend payments, see Committee on Unit Valuation, *Appraisal of Railroad and Other Public Utility Property for Ad Valorem Tax Purposes*, 32–33.

[24] The test could not be made as to telephone rentals in view of the way Moody's Manuals report the data.

[25] The NATA committee would deal with the dividends alone, but one has difficulty in understanding how the method used avoids (if it does) the influence of capitalization structure.

putation of capitalization rates showed significant differences in most cases in the early fifties and in almost no case in the mid-sixties.

It should be perhaps pointed out that the differences between the situation disclosed in the first and the second Kentucky studies were anticipated when it was found that the reliability of the capitalization rates had greatly increased in the time interim which had elapsed. The fact that the reduced error is a significant element in the explanation is supported by the absence of any statistically significant error on any one of these counts in the case of taxpayers showing a distinctly low coefficient of variation.

LOCAL SERVICE CHARGES: *Theory and Practice*

MILTON Z. KAFOGLIS

THIS PAPER attempts to evaluate service charges as a source of municipal revenue. Since a clear-cut definition of "service charges" is difficult to formulate, it is almost impossible to state precisely the quantitative dimensions of their use. In this paper, service charges are defined broadly: they include all payments imposed on a benefit or *quid pro quo* principle provided the payee acquiesces in the payment of the levy. This definition comprehends all payments levied under some variant of the voluntary exchange theory as well as prices which require only market exchange. It is assumed that "taxes" are imposed under a majority-rule political institution, while service charges, if they involve any political action at all, are imposed under a Wicksellian rule of unanimity. Under this formulation, service charges include payments which are not explicitly redistributional but are characteristically voluntary. Taxes, on the other hand, are compulsory levies having redistributional effects. Thus, service charges are associated with allocation, and taxes with redistribution. Service charges can, in turn, be subdivided into "prices" and "price-taxes," the former requiring only market action and the latter requiring collective action in response to externalities. Although other definitions and classifications are possible, this paper relies on this general framework.

The definition of service charges employed by the U.S. Bureau of the Census most closely conforms to what we have described as "prices." [1] In fiscal 1965–66 the category "charges and miscellaneous general revenue" accounted for 22.7 per cent of total locally derived revenues.[2] This category is now second in impor-

---

[1] For a recent survey of the use of service charges see Juan de Torres, *Financing Local Government* (National Industrial Conference Board, 1967), Chapter 5. An earlier but more complete description is Gerald J. Boyle, *Use of Service Charges in Local Government* (National Industrial Conference Board, 1960).

[2] This does not include water and other utility revenue. Inclusion of these items

tance to the property tax as a source of municipal revenue and is the dominant source of locally derived revenue in many communities in the South. Moreover, service charges are increasing at a more rapid rate than other types of local revenue. The trend toward greater reliance on service charges is somewhat more pronounced in the large metropolitan areas which traditionally have relied on such charges to a lesser extent than smaller cities.[3]

The increase in the use of price-like charges by municipal governments has important implications for economic efficiency and equity in urban communities. The appropriate use of pricing mechanisms should encourage a more efficient utilization and development of local service facilities. At the same time, service charges as they frequently are employed by local governments are more regressive than traditional forms of local taxation and their increased use suggests the possibility of a shift in distributive relationships. It is maintained in this paper that the regressive character of service charges is a result of a faulty application of pricing principles which frustrates both efficiency and equity and that appropriate pricing practices would lead to improved efficiency, to superior distributive relationships, and to a diminution in the level of "coercive" taxation. This, in turn, might lead to revenue gains and to an increased tolerance for purely redistributive taxation.

The Scope for Pricing

Municipal governments are essentially service organizations and,

---

increases the proportion to 37.7 per cent of total locally derived revenue. Bureau of the Census, *Local Government Finances in Selected Metropolitan Areas in 1965–66*, Series 6F-No. 14 (Washington, D.C.: Government Printing Office, 1967), 7.

[3] In fiscal 1965–66, thirty-eight selected SMSA's accounting for 53.8 per cent of the nation's locally derived revenue received $3.85 billion in "charges and miscellaneous revenue." This source accounted for 20.8 per cent of locally derived revenue in these major metropolitan areas. The rest of the nation's localities received $4.18 billion in charge revenue accounting for 24.8 per cent of locally derived funds. Whereas charges and miscellaneous revenues for all governments increased by 11.7 per cent from 1964–65 to 1965–66, this source increased by 13.0 per cent in the thirty-eight major SMSA's. *Ibid.*

if national defense is excluded, are responsible for about half of the resource-absorbing activity of all governments in the United States. Therefore, it is exceedingly important that municipal services be provided efficiently. At the same time, municipal services must be financed equitably. It is at this point that benefit and ability-to-pay finance seem at odds. The benefit theory has been criticized as impractical (because measurements of benefit are difficult) and illogical (because the welfare recipient "can't pay his own check"). The problem of measurement applies with equal force in the case of ability-to-pay, involving measurements and interpersonal comparisons of utility at the conceptual level and the determination of taxable income on the basis of a host of exceedingly dubious deductions at the application level. There is no reason to believe that benefits cannot be imputed as effectively as ability-to-pay. Taxable income, of course, is an objective measure, but what does it really mean? Benefits are a more subjective measure, but they do have a real meaning. The basic criticism of benefit taxation must revolve around its distributional effects while its major advantage lies in its allocational effects.

The ensuing discussion attempts to maintain a distinction between distribution and allocation, not on the assumption that the problems are separable, but in order to reveal the nature of the trade-off between equity and efficiency. What solution would emerge if efficiency were the only consideration? What distributional criteria are violated in this solution? How may the two be compromised? These are the questions we wish to discuss.

Economists have had a great deal of difficulty in distinguishing those goods which can be sold from those which cannot be sold and even more difficulty in distinguishing those which should be sold from those which should not. The general rule is that any good can be sold if there are some means of excluding some of the consumers. This not only provides revenue, but reveals consumer preferences and, presumably, should encourage a more efficient allocation of resources. In the case of a purely collective good in the Samuelson sense, exclusion cannot be achieved because each consumer partakes of the indivisible total. Thus, a change in expenditures for national defense affects all consumers "equally" because the safety of one cannot be increased or decreased without having a similar impact on the other. Although exclusion is difficult to achieve, the financing of a collective good through a system of voluntarily accepted price-taxes can be envisioned if there are some means of revealing preferences. In short, if the "free-rider" (consumer who obtains a service or good at zero cost) problem could be overcome, virtually all government services could be sold on either a "cost-of-service" or "value-of-service" principle.[4] And, the most obvious way of handling free-riders is to exclude them. The scope for pricing thus depends on the possibility of revealing preferences, and this in turn depends largely on the ability to exclude.

The means by which exclusion can be achieved are many and varied, depending on organizational, technical, and legal factors. The difference between success or failure for a drive-in theater may depend on the ability to exclude viewers through the erection of a fence; the fence seems to make a difference as to whether the movie is a "private" or "public" good. The classic example of a purely collective good is the lighthouse whose beams are available to all ships. But even in this case, property rights on the sea could

---

[4] R. H. Musgrave in *The Theory of Public Finance* (New York: McGraw-Hill, 1959), 84, criticizes the benefit or voluntary exchange approach on two grounds. First, he contends that this model does not yield a determinate optimum in the Paretian sense. His second criticism is that preferences will not be revealed because it pays to be a free-rider. The first criticism has been rejected by Ansel M. Sharp and Donald R. Escarraz in "A Reconsideration of the Price or Exchange Theory of Public Finance," *Southern Economic Journal*, XXXI (October, 1964), 132–39, on the grounds that Musgrave's technical analysis is in error. The second criticism, *i.e.*, that preferences will not be revealed, has merit but may not apply in many cases. The extent to which individual preferences are revealed depends significantly on the types of fiscal institutions that are employed. Comparative analysis of fiscal institutions is in its infancy. For a discussion of the relation between modern fiscal institutions and individual choice see James M. Buchanan, *Public Finance in Democratic Process* (Chapel Hill: University of North Carolina Press, 1967). If institutions which encourage revealed choices are inefficient or rejected on some other grounds, the theory fails as an explanation of a politico-economic process; but it does not fail as a means for analyzing tax allocations or as a means for conceptualizing the benefit theory of taxation.

be defined in such a way that ships could be excluded. Similarly, otherwise free television signals can be sold for a price if descramblers are employed. Even the services of an air raid siren could be marketed if there were some means of channeling the warning to some, but not to others. The fact that there are alternative means of organizing the supply of a good suggests that the choice between "free" services and services to be sold is largely a matter of selecting the most efficient organization. The factors which condition this institutional choice have not been discovered, described, and classified as yet. Although various components of the problem like externalities, joint supply, unit size, overhead, and zero marginal cost have received separate treatment in the light of particular problems, a general theory of public goods supply continues to elude us.[5] We have no choice but to grope along with the fragments that are available.

Education and Health Services

Educational, health, and fire protection services can be sold for a price because the exclusion principle can be made to apply. The case for tax-financing in such instances rests either on redistributional considerations or on externalities. Consider education. Assuming that all incomes were either equal or "just" and that the choice available to the family were whether to pay a fee or a tax, the balance would probably swing in favor of the fee, especially if there were a choice of schools. Education could be provided either publicly or privately, under appropriate minimum criteria, and parents could select freely among alternatives. The basic problem in this solution is that unless education is made compulsory all children will not be sent to school, and the externalities associated with education will not be fully exploited. However, the fact that a service is made compulsory does not prevent the use of fees, charges, and prices. Nor does the use of compulsion necessarily imply a distributive judgment calling for tax-financing. Laws

[5] Significant progress along these lines has been made by James M. Buchanan, especially in *The Demand and Supply of Public Goods* (Chicago: Rand-McNally, 1968).

requiring compulsory annual inspection of automobile brakes at a service charge are not novel. Individuals are sometimes required to pay for such inspections at a private garage, and the law is enforced through a system of windshield stickers. Health certificates signed by a family physician are sometimes a requisite for school enrollments as well as for the purchase of a marriage license. In a collective decision individuals might unanimously agree that compulsion should be employed in the case of certain services like immunization, education, and automobile and fire inspection. They might also agree unanimously that each individual could select his own supplier. Certainly, there is less compulsion and possibly greater efficiency in this arrangement than to impose both a compulsory tax and the source of supply. The fact that after reaching such agreements in a collective context the individual may go to considerable trouble to avoid honoring them does not contradict the view that such agreements conform to Paretian welfare criteria.[6] Thus, if the exclusion principle can be made to apply, a purely collective demand can be satisfied and financed on a service charge basis. It may often be more convenient for a government agency to provide the service, but this requires no change in pricing principles. Thus, a "cost-of-service" application of the benefit theory is relevant where exclusion is possible. In the case that has been described, the key to exclusion is the physical divisibility of the service. Fees paid to government for services that individuals are "compelled" to purchase can be based on sound pricing principles. Compelled purchases of this sort lead to a paradoxical situation: consumer sovereignty in the usual sense is violated but individual welfare in the Paretian sense is enhanced. In any case, taxation in the traditional sense and government resource using activity are not essential to the attainment of collective objectives.

The essence of the "compelled purchaser" model is mutual

[6] For an analysis of the "compelled purchaser" model see my *Welfare Economics and Subsidy Programs* (Gainesville: University of Florida Press, 1962), 28–40. The key to this model is that although there may be no market demand expressed for a service which yields reciprocal externalities, the individual in a collective context will agree to purchase the item provided others also do so.

recognition of the interdependence created by externality. In short, externalities are reciprocal, and unanimous agreement can be achieved in a mutual gains through trading framework. In many instances, such symmetrical relationships do not exist. The externalities are relevant to one person, but not to the other, and the basis for trading may be more obscure. An example of this relationship is found in urban transportation where the motorist has an interest in mass transportation which reduces congestion and other highway costs. Such a situation is depicted in Figure 1 where D_a represents the private demand for bus transportation, P, the bus fare and Q, the number of passengers transported by bus. The line D_s represents the savings (in time and frustration)

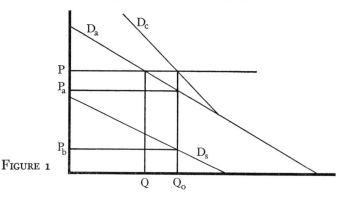

FIGURE 1

that accrue to private motorists as a function of the number of persons who ride the bus. The collective demand is D_c (the sum of D_a and D_s over quantities of bus transportation) which calls for a greater use of the bus system. One solution is to reduce the bus fare to P_a and to collect the balance (P_b per bus trip) from motorists and other indirect beneficiaries either through a specific bus charge (in much the same way as sewerage systems are sometimes financed), increased highway user charges, or through general taxation. Thus, many services may be financed partially through prices and partially through other charges and taxes. In such cases prices can be based on a "value-of-service" or benefits-received principle whereas in the case of completely "compelled pur-

170

chases" a "cost-of-service" criterion is appropriate. Of course, individuals could be compelled to ride the bus (say, by denying motoring privileges to all but a few), but this solution requires coercive allocation of rights and privileges similar in character to redistributional taxation and is not consistent with any reasonable interpretation of service charge theory.

The provision of subsidized services as in the case of mass transportation is not always in response to externality. Sometimes prices are reduced to a level below cost of service because they seem "too high." This is obviously in response to distributional considerations and is irrational in the absence of such considerations. Thus, the idea that water should be "cheap" has led to low water rates and increased property taxes with very dubious distributional effects. For the "median" taxpayer the choice is either high prices for the service or high taxes to recover the loss imposed by low prices. In the absence of a sound externality argument, the high price is superior on efficiency grounds. The attempt to grapple with the distributional problem through price adjustments may create confusion and conflict with little improvement in equity unless it is employed with exceedingly great care.

Health services are frequently offered free or at nominal service charges. Again, if the distributional question were not a factor, the "compelled purchaser" solution could be employed in the presence of the reciprocal externalities which characterize communicable disease. However, if sufficient agreement to employ this model cannot be achieved, some variant of the subsidy solution depicted in Figure 1 involving a combination of prices and taxes may be necessary. And, of course, administrative considerations may dictate that vaccines, chest x-rays, and the like be free. Collecting charges also involves costs which must be weighed against the gains from pricing.

Free or partially subsidized health services in the absence of relevant externalities represent a response to a distributional problem. The idea that everyone should be able to afford health service is more an argument for improved income distribution than for free services. Be that as it may, free services seem easier to attain politically than the necessary or desirable distribution of income. The great danger is the illusion that free services are really free and that they may, therefore, be used with no regard to cost. In the case of health and education, the supply of these services is under the trusteeship of professionals, and the waste may not be great. However, to ensure an effective pressure to economize, it is necessary to keep facilities overcrowded and to rely on professional rationing rather than on market rationing. The welfare state seems an inefficient solution to the problem of income distribution. Although the result is inefficient, at least from the point of view of those consumers who would rather pay and not have to wait in line, it may represent a reasonable compromise in the absence of a more general solution concerning income distribution. At the same time, even if income distribution were adequate, there is no assurance that individuals would voluntarily purchase education and health in the "correct" amounts. To the extent that reciprocal externalities are present, the compelled purchaser solution could be employed, and in the presence of nonreciprocal externalities the subsidy solution would be appropriate. Thus, income redistribution tied to compelled purchases represents an alternative solution to the welfare state. The obvious difficulty with this solution is that it may be difficult to achieve the degree of unanimity required by the model. Compelled purchases under a system of majority rule are probably less acceptable than the welfare state.

The problems created by "free" services are especially pronounced in higher education. It is not clear that equal opportunity requires free service. The majority of college students come from families which can well afford to pay tuition fees, and those who do not can be granted scholarships and loans to complete their education. In the case of higher education, the distributional argument is especially weak because state sales tax systems tend to be regressive and higher education is consumed in the main by upper income classes. Thus, the individual who lives in the ghetto may have second thoughts about that extra two-cent cigarette tax earmarked for university buildings. Significantly, the greatest objections to increased fees have come from educators and parents of college-bound students rather than from those who really don't have an equal opportunity.

A similar, but probably less severe, distributional situation exists at the primary and secondary level. Slums and ghettos produce property tax revenue (more than may be commonly supposed), but the best facilities are built in the suburbs. In some instances it is even possible that the net effect created by the system of local school finance redistributes income from low-income to high-income classes. In any event, a question may be raised as to whether free education creates much in the way of a desirable redistribution. It is not clear that the existence of a poverty-stricken segment in the population calls for a global policy of free education. It may be (though a proof has not been forthcoming) that a free school system is the most efficient means for educating children—in one way or another they will all go to school—but the usual redistributional, equal opportunity, and other ideological arguments that confuse the development of sound educational policy have very little to do with the selection of the most efficient institutions for financing education. Increased experimentation with fees has lightened the burden of the general taxpayer in many school districts. One objection to this approach is that some children will receive a better education than others. However, this need not be the case because minimum criteria can be imposed and low-income students can still be sent to the best schools with a public subsidy. The idea that all children should have the same education has an appeal in a democracy, but it is as much an argument for reducing the quality of education as for increasing it.

Police Services and Fire Protection

Police services and fire protection are financed through the use of general fund revenues. Since some quantity of private police and fire protection would surely emerge in the absence of public provision, these services also create the possibility of charge revenue. Indeed, there are instances of private fire protection where the individual pays a monthly or annual "fire charge." The exclusion principle can be made to apply by refusing to serve those who have not made a payment. The maximum payment that any individual would be willing to make can be determined by calculating the expected loss during any particular payment period. A similar actuarial calculation could be employed to determine a lump sum charge that would be paid in the event of an actual outbreak of fire. Two actuarially equivalent contracts are possible —one based on periodic payments, the other on a lump sum payment at the time of fire. Because of the greater risk of nonpayment in the case of the lump sum, the discount rate would be exceedingly high. Indeed, the lump sum could exceed the value of the property, in which case it would not be selected. The individual who does not select one contract or the other simply places no value on fire protection. However, a self-insuror or gambler of this sort may impose external costs on others. In this particular case, the individual may become a welfare burden and others may lose any "surplus" values that he is currently providing. Assuming these external relations are reciprocal, the "compelled purchases" model can be made to apply. The compelled purchases solution is especially likely where houses are close together and the externalities are more obvious. In this case, the solution is likely to be a compulsory fire charge based on the expected loss during any particular period. Assessment directly according to value of property and inversely according to proximity to the fire station is a likely fiscal outcome. The solution may be similar in many respects to that achieved under current property tax financing.

However, it is doubtful that fire protection services are efficiently organized in many parts of the United States. The fact that tax payments are not closely related to benefits probably has led to excessive investment in fire protection. Suppose, for example, that fire protection costs were imposed on fire insurance

174

companies or alternatively that local governments became insurors. What arrangement of fire protection would be consistent with premium or cost minimization? The attempt to minimize fire loss would surely lead to the establishment of fire departments operated by the insuror. However, a more complete balancing of fire protection costs against the risk of fire loss would be encouraged with reorganization of fire protection a likely possibility. Under public financing, the individual is frequently confronted with higher fire insurance rates unless additional public fire protection facilities are provided. Under prevailing institutions the individual, the fire insurance companies, and the local fire department will exert pressure for expanded fire-fighting facilities. The individual, as taxpayer, may not be represented at all, especially if he assumes that public services come at zero cost to him, that is, if he hopes to be or thinks he is a free-rider. Whether he will, in fact, make this assumption depends on his awareness of the tax implications to him; and these implications depend, in turn, on the criterion of tax equity that is employed. If he assumes public facilities come at zero cost to him, or underestimates his tax share, fire protection facilities will be overextended, at least in terms of economic efficiency.

Police protection is exceedingly difficult to analyze because jointness exists on both the supply and demand side. A unit of police protection controls traffic, protects property, and enforces a wide variety of laws, some of which yield purely collective benefits while others yield narrowly private benefits. Conceptually, these joint outputs could be priced in the same manner as petroleum products or beef and hides—that is, in accordance with demand elasticities for the separate services. However, the pervasive externalities on the consumption side and the difficulty of efficiently applying an exclusion principle limit the possibility of service charge financing. Certainly, the voluntary exchange or benefit theory can be applied in an analytical sense, but the indivisibility of benefits among individuals probably would lead to bargaining and to the "free-rider" problem.

At the same time, separate charges for police services are possible. A large proportion of police costs are associated with traffic congestion. A number of economists have noted that the institutions for financing motor transportation do not fully reflect the real cost of motoring. The possibility of financing some of these costs through the highway user tax structure, as in the case of state highway patrols, merits consideration. Another feature of law enforcement is that the process of enforcement creates revenue in the form of fines and penalties. In some communities law enforcement is a money-making business appreciated especially by out-of-state speeders. In a medium-sized, "progressive" community with which this writer is familiar, approximately 30 per cent of police costs are recovered in police court. Criminals pay their own way to a greater extent than is commonly supposed. The ghetto, of course, is a burden to all taxpayers, but it is also a fairly lucrative source of police revenue.

A considerable portion of police service lends itself to private financing. The restaurateur's "free lunch" for the policeman on the beat is a payment for more than his "share" of police protection. The private competition for such free services suggests that even the most collective of goods has a private price. Special police details to handle the traffic at athletic events impose specific costs, and the benefits accrue to a specific group of individuals. In some municipalities the sponsors of such events are expected to hire city policemen; in other cases a payment is made directly to the city. The use of free police services in these instances is neither efficient nor equitable. However, there is an administrative cost in the collection of such charges as well as a decision-making cost in their determination; in some cases charges will prove economic; in others, they will not.

The cumbersome nature of service charges is clearly an important efficiency consideration, but the equity notion that it is "all in one pocket, out the other" or that it all evens out in the long run has not been demonstrated. Indeed, it is possible that a greater reliance on the *quid pro quo* in the case of police services would either reduce the local tax burden of the low-income classes or lead to revisions in the attitude that "if everyone were like me, we would have no policemen."

Recreational Facilities

Free or partially free provision of recreational facilities is based either on external effects or on distributional considerations. Where relevant external effects are present, the use of pricing devices may restrict the development and use of these facilities to levels below optimum. In such cases, either free or partially subsidized services may be desirable. However, if the demand for such facilities is highly inelastic to price, the use of prices will not significantly reduce the amount of service taken, and the pricing policy can be evaluated primarily in terms of its distributional effects. In many instances it is likely that inelastic demands are associated with those who have ability-to-pay. Distributional considerations, for example, probably are of little concern in the case of those who are able to attend national and state parks. The major economic argument for free entrance in such instances is that short-run marginal cost is zero, and even this argument loses much of its force when demands are inelastic since entrance fees may not reduce the number of visitors. On the other hand, if demands are elastic, the case for low or zero prices in the presence of zero marginal cost is persuasive. The unrecovered overhead or burden that arises as a result of a zero price policy takes on the characteristics of a purely collective good to those who use the service and may be financed through taxes levied according to ability-to-pay or voluntary-exchange principles, price discrimination, or other means which do not stifle the use of the facility.[7] The various alternatives for financing overheads

---

[7] As a theoretical matter, lump sum payments are most appropriate for financing losses due to marginal cost pricing. The other alternatives violate Paretian criteria in one way or another. This paper does not espouse a rigid adherence to Paretian criteria. Nevertheless, the Paretian framework is employed because it is analytically useful and is capable of providing useful insights about the nature of policy problems. As a general rule, it is not capable of specifying a practical solution, but its use may forestall the types of mistakes sometimes made by practical and political men.

have different distributional effects and carry implications to long-run development decisions. Appropriate methods of finance should be established at the time the original benefit-cost ratio is calculated and the investment decision is made.

Where facilities are overcrowded, marginal costs are not zero, even when additional money costs are not involved. Congestion creates delay and deterioration in the quality of service. In the absence of distributional considerations, price rationing may improve the efficiency of overcrowded facilities. However, if the facilities serve both rich and poor alike, distributional policy may reject price rationing and cause each patron to pay a price by waiting longer and receiving less service. The costs of congestion cannot be avoided; it is simply a matter of how they should be borne. The essentials of the congestion problem were described by A. C. Pigou in his classic comparison of the distribution of traffic between free roads and toll roads. The problem is illustrated

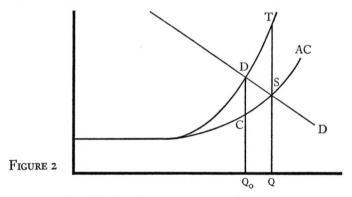

FIGURE 2

in Figure 2 which depicts a facility like a park, recreation hall, museum, or highway.[8] The individual incurs certain private costs in utilizing the facility even when it is free—the major cost usually being time. As the facility becomes crowded, these private costs rise, as depicted by AC, the cost which each individual must bear

[8] Figure 2 is adopted from Herbert D. Mohring, "Relation Between Optimum Congestion Tolls and Present Highway User Charges," *Highway Research Record*, No. 47 (Washington, 1964).

at various levels of utilization. If demand is D, the facility will serve Q patrons per day. Each individual will equate his demand to the private cost (AC) which he must bear. He will not consider that his decision will affect the private costs of all other patrons. If the delays imposed on others were considered, the marginal cost of his decision is the distance QT which exceeds private cost by ST, the cost imposed on others. Paretian optimal use of the facility requires Q_o patrons, and this can be achieved by a charge or toll equal to CD. It can be shown that those who remain on the facility and pay the toll will more than compensate for those who are driven off.

Whether such a price policy would reduce congestion depends partly on demand elasticity. If the demand is relatively inelastic, imposition of the charge will not greatly affect utilization of the facility, although it will provide a means of finance and impose costs in such a way that they are clearly recognizable by those who impose them. The use of the charge when demand is relatively inelastic will result in the individual's bearing both the charge and the congestion. However, if the funds are used to expand the facility, the congestion will diminish and net gains will accrue as a result of the price policy.[9] If the facility is not expanded, the charge becomes equivalent to rent, and its extraction must be evaluated on distributional grounds. Where demands are relatively elastic, congestion pricing can be very effective.

The overwhelming difficulty with congestion pricing, its efficiency notwithstanding, is that it may drive low-income persons off the facility. Unless a means of compensation is developed, the gains accrue to those who pay the tolls while those who are priced out sustain losses. Without compensation, crowding of a free facility may be better on distributional grounds notwithstanding the increased efficiency associated with price rationing. The danger in abandoning price rationing is that pressures will develop for expanding the facility in order to eliminate congestion com-

---

[9] Mohring, "Relation Between Optimum Congestion Tolls and Present Highway User Charges."

pletely. However, use on the basis of a zero short-run price is excessive in terms of the long-run horizon. In short, excess demand or congestion of free facilities should be a permanent state of affairs for the same reason that there is a permanent excess demand for free lollipops.

Neighborhood parks, swimming pools, or recreation halls may be priced or not priced depending on many factors, some of which have been described. A crowded swimming pool in a low-income neighborhood might be made "free" in the light of externalities, distribution, and demand elasticity while a not-so-crowded swimming pool in the suburbs could be priced because of the absence of these factors. The solution would depend on externalities, distributional questions, demand elasticities, and a host of other considerations. The point is that public provision should not carry the implication of zero cost. Simply because all children should be able to swim in the summer does not mean that general taxation and free entry is the most desirable financing institution.

Public Utility Services

Local governments provide a wide variety of public utility type services—water, electricity, sewerage, refuse collection. Sewerage and refuse collections are sometimes financed through general revenues, sometimes through service charges and special assessments, and sometimes through a combination of revenue sources. Both services are characterized by reciprocal externality and conform reasonably well to the "compelled purchaser" model.

The case for price rationing in the case of sewerage services applies in the case of industrial and commercial users who have alternative means of waste disposal. Price rationing, which requires metering, is especially significant for growing communities which have continuous pressures on sewage treatment plants. Insofar as residential services are concerned, metering of waste may not be worth the cost, especially in the light of the relatively inelastic demand. However, it is important that the fixed cost of the distribution system be reflected in a manner that encourages economic location of residential and business property. Distribution costs rise as the distance from the treatment plant increases, and a system of uniform charges may fail to reflect the impact of alternative locations on service costs. Many communities impose surcharges for service outside the city limits, partly because of the higher cost of service and partly in the light of alleged suburban exploitation of the core city. However, areas within the city, but at a distance from the treatment plant, are at an advantage where uniform charges are employed. Since demands are relatively inelastic after the service is installed, the case for short-run price rationing is weak. Demands are more elastic at the time a location is selected and before the service is installed. Since all charges are considered when a location is selected, the "full cost" of facilities and operation should be reflected in the charge structure.

Monthly sewerage charges are sometimes made on a flat fee or near flat fee per house basis, thus making all locations equally desirable, at least from the point of view of these services. Charges in accordance with water consumption are also common and have the advantage of reflecting treatment costs. Since water and sewerage costs tend to vary together for each consumption unit, there is much to be said for pricing the entire package under a single rate schedule.

The difficulty with the flat rate per house basis is best illustrated by the monthly charge for refuse collection. In most instances the flat charge leads to a subsidy to the suburban areas and a penalty on the densely populated urban areas. The costs of refuse collection in a locale where homes are densely packed or where there are housing complexes are much lower than the costs incurred in suburban areas where lots are large and distances great. Thus, prices which vary more realistically with distance, size of lot and number of garbage cans might encourage improved locational decisions. Of course, a single small charge does not determine a housing decision, but there are many such charges and they add up to a significant total. If individuals reckon with a more accurate estimate of the costs these charges impose, they might find an advantage in smaller lots, apartments, and housing complexes. From a distributional point of view flat fees penalize the small homeowner relative to the large, the city relative to the suburb, and possibly the low-income classes relative to the high-income classes.

The use of property taxation for financing sewerage and refuse collection services may yield a distribution of burdens similar to cost-of-service pricing. After a location decision is made, the impact of sophisticated pricing on resource use would probably be minimal. If the impact of pricing is not significant, the use of charges for sewerage and refuse collection may not be worth the trouble and property taxation might seem more appropriate. An additional factor that might encourage the use of property taxation rather than service charges is the deductibility of property taxes for income tax purposes. For the person in a high income tax bracket, the property tax is advantageous compared to a properly determined service charge. The costs of administering periodic service charges in the case of refuse collection and sewerage, along with the present misdirected income tax advantage, may tip the scales in favor of general finance. On the other hand, the costs of administering a system of charges through a central office which issues a monthly itemized bill may not be especially great. The flat fee per house is undesirable on almost all grounds and is identical to the poll tax in its distributional effects.

The use of faulty pricing policies in the case of water supply has contributed to the serious water supply problem now confronting the nation's major metropolitan areas. The usual block rate structure employed in the pricing of water and electricity results in a declining rate per gallon or kilowatt hour as usage increases. If the decline in the rate is greater than the decline in the cost-of-service, the result will be an excessive "quantity discount." There are two implications to this characteristic of water and electricity rates. First, profits made on services rendered to small users are used to cover losses incurred in serving large users.

Second, if the service is in short supply, as it is in the case of water, it seems illogical to deliberately promote its greater use. Like certain fiscal institutions, rate structures can make goods seem cheaper than they really are. This problem is aggravated by the existence of off-peak and on-peak use. For example, the design capacity of a water distribution system is determined by peak demand which usually occurs in August. From a theoretical point of view, the highest rates should be charged during the August peak, thus discouraging wasteful uses during the peak period and encouraging a smaller investment. This, of course, conforms to everyday business practice. Tickets to Sunday night baseball games cost more than tickets to Wednesday afternoon games. Matinee prices are below evening prices. These are sound pricing practices which businessmen understand, but which somehow seem beyond the comprehension of some municipal authorities. The peak load in water comsumption occurs in August when suburbanites are watering their lawns. At this peak period they are paying (under present rate schedules) the year's lowest average rate per gallon and receive a "discount" on each additional gallon used, thus encouraging even further use at a time when the system is already overloaded. The consulting engineer who makes a study and concludes that investment in the water distribution system ought to be expanded may be in serious error. It is possible that appropriate rate adjustments can cope with the situation. In the case of water, it might be desirable to have a flat fee for some minimum amount coupled with a rate that increases with water usage, especially in the summer months. This could serve to ameliorate a critical water shortage. Since water is associated with cleanliness and sanitation, the minimum amount might be offered free in order to satisfy these externalities. At the present time the most costly water to produce is sprinkled on lawns. Present rates also work to the economic advantage of the suburbs, may encourage uneconomic location, and impose excessive burdens on small users.

The whole concept of promotional utility rate-making merits

careful re-examination in the light of economic and equity considerations. There is a tendency among engineers and long-range planners to project needs without even a passing reference to the rate structure. Projected population is multiplied by projected per capita usage to arrive at an estimate of future needs. Implicit in these projections is the use of a promotional pricing system which may not have a sound economic rationale. Does it not seem odd to employ promotional prices at a time when resources are scarce and communities have dramatic capital shortage in other areas?

Service Charges in Perspective

The recent increase in the use of service charges by municipal governments has important implications to economic efficiency and to equity in urban communities. Although service charges are an important source of local revenue and one which has not been fully exploited, their basic purpose is to encourage efficient use and development of municipal service organizations. Where they are ineffective as allocative devices, the cost of collection will frequently eliminate them as a practical source of revenue. However, the use of the service charge, if only as a bookkeeping device, will discourage the illusion that public services are really free. The cost accounting required by service charges may seem cumbersome, but it provides precisely the type of information local officials and citizens need in making budgetary decisions.

The service charge brings the individual into a much closer and more specific relation with the local government—a condition generally considered desirable in a democracy. Generalized discussions concerning whose ox is being gored tend to become emotional and ideological; the service charge provides a firm and specific basis for rational debate.

The major shortcoming of cost-of-service finance lies in its distributional implications. There is at least a hint that cost-of-service finance may turn out to be less regressive than traditional local finance. Although much research remains to be done before the distributional implications of service charge finance can be assessed fully, it has been suggested that in some communities increased reliance on cost-of-service finance might ameliorate the condition of the low-income classes. Promotional utility rates and flat rates per house are especially suspect since they encourage inefficiency and lead to service rate structures that are more regressive in their effects than the property tax. The distributional problem created by service charges may be due to faulty pricing practices rather than to a faculty principle. If service charge finance is to be employed, it is exceedingly important that it not be used as a means of collecting from those "who do not pay other taxes." This logic usually leads to an improperly calculated price. In arguing the case for more equitable service charges before a city commission, this writer discovered that flat charges are viewed by some politicians as a means of "offsetting" the progressive federal income tax. Thus, from the point of view of the low-income person, the progressive federal tax may yield a curious mixture of blessings.

Service charges are usually determined hurriedly and politically under the pressure of having to raise enough revenue, and little attention is usually given to their impact on economic efficiency and equity. Since service rate structures, like tax structures, are difficult to alter once they are established, it is important that local authorities and citizen groups be aware of the potential economic effects of various types of rate structures when making such decisions.

The need for criteria and guidelines for the establishment of service rate structures is even more urgent in the light of core-city decline and programs for urban renewal, redevelopment, and model cities. Uneconomic and inequitable service rate structures can hamper the attainment of the objectives of these programs. Moreover, these programs provide an excellent opportunity for review of the existing structure of charges.

The order of priorities in this area of local finance would appear to call for review and overhaul of existing service rate structures before a search is initiated for new sources of charge revenue.

While the recent increase in the use of these charges offers new opportunities for experiments in local finance, it also creates the possibility that the service charge may be viewed as a revenue device rather than as an allocative device. In this case, the redistributions of income that occur may result in a more regressive structure of local finance than exists under traditional forms of taxation.

CONTRIBUTORS

Arthur P. Becker is professor of economics, University of Wisconsin, Milwaukee.

Joseph M. Bonin is associate professor of economics, Auburn University.

James M. Buchanan is professor of economics, University of Virginia.

C. H. Donovan is professor of economics, University of Florida.

Milton Z. Kafoglis is professor of finance, University of Tennessee.

Arthur D. Lynn, Jr., is professor of economics and associate dean of faculties, Ohio State University.

James W. Martin is emeritus professor of economics, University of Kentucky.

Dick Netzer is professor of public finance, Graduate School of Public Administration, New York University.

William D. Ross is dean of the College of Business Administration, Louisiana State University.

John Shannon is assistant director, Advisory Commission on Intergovernmental Relations.

Elsie M. Watters is director of State-Local Research, Tax Foundation, Inc.

Deil S. Wright is professor of political science, University of North Carolina, Chapel Hill.

INDEX